POLITICS IS PEOPLE

"I have had many strange and some bitter experiences in my political life."

SIR ROBERT MENZIES

By the same author

LILACS OUT OF THE DEAD LAND (*poems*)

POLITICS
IS
PEOPLE

The Men of the Menzies Era

EDGAR HOLT

ANGUS AND ROBERTSON

First published in 1969 by

ANGUS & ROBERTSON LTD

221 George Street, Sydney
54 Bartholomew Close, London
107 Elizabeth Street, Melbourne
65 High Street, Singapore

© *Edgar Holt 1969*

National Library of Australia
REGISTRY NUMBER AUS 69-362

SBN 207 95170 5

Registered in Australia for transmission by post as a book
PRINTED IN AUSTRALIA BY HALSTEAD PRESS, SYDNEY

Foreword

"Politics is people" is an old saying. In a literal
way, too, people in politics are more interesting,
as part of the human scene, than politics in
people. I had in mind to attempt a sketch in
words of Sir Robert Menzies, the man, but
quickly discovered that I could not wholly
divorce him from political events or from many
of his contemporaries in politics. So what began
as a sketch portrait grew into a gallery and a very
condensed account of political affairs and campaigns since 1934.

EDGAR HOLT

Contents

Introductory Thought on Part One

The best that can be hoped from any government is that it will navigate among unknown
rocks and unexpected hurricanes without sinking
the ship and drowning the crew.

JOYCE CARY

Part One

EARLY YEARS
IN THE JUNGLE

I

A Background for the Hero

WHEN Robert Gordon Menzies descended upon Canberra in 1934 it was a little community of 6,000 people. Travel to this remote capital was by slow train or car. Civic Centre, where the local inhabitants did their shopping, seemed far away from Parliament House and looked like a Hollywood set for a Western. Politicians walking from the Hotel Canberra would occasionally be attacked by nesting magpies. When winter fogs blotted out the landscape, people who knew the place well lost themselves. In those days the great host of public servants had not invaded Canberra. Tourists were few. The capital was not a rendezvous for conventions. There was no lake, no bridges. Canberra's academic world was small, its diplomatic community was small, the amenities of civilized living were slight. Rare, one-night stands in the Albert Hall tentatively introduced the theatre and the arts.

Like the city itself the business of government in 1934 was also relatively small. Presiding over it, amiable and not unlike a caricature of a koala, was Joseph Aloysius Lyons, Prime Minister of Australia. He had been translated to the office by way of Tasmania, the Australian Labor Party, and the Depression. Greatness had been thrust upon him. A few years earlier he had been a minister in the Scullin Government, but not until early 1931 did the name Lyons mean very much to the Australian electorate. Australia was deep in the Depression and men without work walked the streets, desperate and bewildered. It was a bitter as well as a hungry time. There were some who looked to Prime Minister Scullin for help and guidance and to his Treasurer, that powerful and able Labor leader, Edward Granville Theodore. They had not yet turned to the genial Tasmanian, Joe Lyons. Perhaps it was an accident of history that Lyons became Acting Treasurer from 25th August 1930 to 10th January 1931, while Scullin and Theodore were across the seas at the Imperial Conference. Whether this transition was capricious or in the stars, it led on to a confrontation that changed the course of politics. Put down baldly, Lyons disagreed with his leader on policy. In quiet and mellow times this might have had little consequence; in the dangerous climate of 1930 the disagreement led to Lyons's resignation from the Scullin Ministry. The sequel is written in the political history of the 'thirties. Suddenly and emotionally Joseph Aloysius Lyons becomes the head and front of a campaign to save Australia. He talks to Australia as the voice of what is called the All for Australia Movement.

It is relevant to this story to remember that in October 1929 the Bruce-Page Government had been destroyed. Arbitration was the issue, but the fact of political life for the Government's backers was that the Melbourne Establishment, personified in the immaculate figure of Stanley Melbourne Bruce, had been rejected. In such aristocratic refuges as the Melbourne Club and in the board room of the Melbourne *Argus* this was a shattering revelation of democracy's limitations. Simple students of the contemporary political scene may not understand that in the days of the decline and fall of the Bruce-Page Government, and for a long time after, only the Australian Labor Party possessed a political organization with roots among the electors. Those who voted "anti-Labor" or "non-Labor", to use the jargon of the time, had no political organization on which to lean, or to influence. Mysterious juntas in Melbourne and Sydney found the money to fight

2

political campaigns and found the political leaders. They discovered Lyons, used him, and promoted him.

Since the fall of the Bruce-Page Government the word Nationalist had lost its political magic. Whatever mystique it ever had was provided by W. M. Hughes, who (let us concede over the brandy and cigars) was also a Labor rebel. The political set-up was obvious and exciting. Marry Lyons to the Nationalists and give them the collective name of the United Australia Party. It was a potent formula in the climate of despair and disillusionment and on 6th January 1932 Lyons was sworn in as Prime Minister.

Observe him now, in 1934, the first Prime Minister under whom Robert Gordon Menzies served. The country is climbing out of the Depression, still a little punch-drunk but more concerned with getting back to economic sanity than with the ambitions of Adolf Hitler. We are a baby country at the bottom of the world and the sun has not yet set on the British Empire. Prime Minister Lyons is midway between the perils of 1931 and the perils of 1939. He has created for himself what we now call an image. He is genial and bland and the perfect family man.

Now let us look at one or two others who adorned the political stage at the time of Menzies' debut. Just the names for the moment so that we may have before us a cast of characters. They will play an important part in the shaping of the political personality of Robert Gordon Menzies.

First to take a bow is Earle Christmas Grafton Page, to whom we are indebted, if the word is apt, for the appearance of the Country Party on the Australian political stage. He takes the first bow in this gallery because he struck the blow that destroyed the Hughes Government in 1923. He will live in this story to strike other blows. He stands before us smiling and giggling, for he was adept at concealing his intentions behind a giggle.

Enter now the gnome-like figure of William Morris Hughes, already a legend. He is to remain on stage for more than a decade and is already a part of history. Although his creative years were deep in the yesterdays he retained a talent for destruction. He had helped with waspish and fierce words to bring down the Bruce-Page Government.

Already, then, we see on stage characters with a fine talent for pulling down. Later we may take breath to analyse this. It is sufficient at this stage to say that we are not looking at a political party as we now understand the word or even at a coalition. We see a gallery of avid individualists conducting their political battles with, as Winston Churchill once said, a fine eighteenth century vigour.

By 1934 Stanley Melbourne Bruce had vanished from the Australian political scene. His departure was not widely mourned. The most prejudiced admirer could not have described him as a typical Australian. In the years of his prime ministership the cartoonists hugely enjoyed decorating him with toppers and spats. Those were days before image-making had become a conscious operation of political propagandists. Nevertheless, the cartoonists, aided by Bruce, imposed upon the Australian elector of the times an Upper Class vision repugnant to an Australia still emerging from its colonial state of mind.

Bruce was unfortunate in following Hughes as Prime Minister. The elegant Bruce, who seemed, but was not, more English than the English, had been decorated and wounded in World War I, but it would have been indecent to dub him "the Little Digger", a description worn by Hughes as flamboyantly as the Digger hat that fell over his enormous ears on Anzac Day. The Australian electorate took Hughes to its arms; it held Bruce at arm's length. However, he plays a small part in the political drama enacted a few years after Menzies' debut.

It is also appropriate to introduce at this stage the handsome, immaculate Richard Gardiner Casey. He looked like a guards officer and spoke with the kind of accent that in England caused members of the lower classes to understand their place and stay in it. His voice and his appearance were not calculated in those days to endear him to the mob. He was rich. This also was of dubious political value to the gallant soldier who in 1931 had moved easily and gracefully to the House of Representatives by way of Corio, where graziers and the

4

Victorian gentry were not unknown. Naturally, he was ambitious. It did not seem remarkable to him that his rise was rapid. He was Assistant Treasurer in the Lyons Ministry as early as 1933. In the year Menzies went to Canberra Casey had also served as Acting Minister for External Affairs. He was to become Treasurer in 1935. So he was an exalted figure in the Lyons hierarchy and the trend of later events suggested that he had hopes of becoming more exalted.

The Lyons Ministry became a coalition between the United Australia Party (which could not have been created without the Lyons crusade leading to Scullin's downfall) and the Country Party (which would not have made its impact without the determination and tenacity of Earle Page). Like most governments it was not uniformly talented. There were bright boys and dull boys. They had self-interest as well as the national interest to serve and when struggles for power began they were all involved in some way.

However, for the time being the stage is occupied by Prime Minister Lyons, supported by the improbable male chorus of Earle Page, W. M. Hughes, Stanley Melbourne Bruce and R. G. Casey. This charming invention is designed to provide a background for the hero, or, if you like, the villain. Enter now, with an appropriate fanfare, Robert Gordon Menzies.

II

Days of Noble Simplicity

THERE'S a story, whether true or false matters not, that the headmaster of the Jeparit State School presented young Menzies with a prize as dux of the fourth grade and said, "Robert, you'll be Prime Minister of Australia." This portrait of a Prime Minister as a small boy is introduced only as a contrast to what some of the older, wickeder boys inhabiting the Canberra jungle probably thought as they shook hands with the newcomer: "Bob, you'll *not* be Prime Minister of Australia."

Advancing on Canberra at the age of thirty-nine he was formidable physically and mentally. His colleagues in Canberra knew what he had done in Victoria. Did they think Prime Minister Lyons had temporarily lost touch with the realities of politics when he invited Menzies to contest the Federal seat of Kooyong in the by-election to follow the retirement of the sitting member, Sir John Latham? Offered a seat, the Victorian barrister was also promised the attorney-generalship.

He was big, handsome, brilliant. He was ambitious. He did not impress as a lovable type some of those who sourly scrutinized him. He had come up the hard way, without family influence in high places, without money. No silver spoon decorated his baby mouth. Not one of the stately homes of Victoria, his birthplace was a tiny, dusty, wheat township with the comical name of Jeparit. His father, James Menzies, had been a coach-painter at Ballarat and a small storekeeper at Jeparit. Young Bob's maternal grandfather was a good Labor man who had helped W. G. Spence to form the first miners' union in Victoria. He poured Labor propaganda into one of his grandson's ears only to discover that it came out of the other. On his father's side the grandparents were Scots. His mother's family came from Cornwall. Although his blood came from the free-booters of the north and the smugglers of Cornwall, he had hard lessons to learn in faraway Canberra.

By now everybody with more than a passing interest in politics knows that Robert Gordon Menzies moved on from the little Jeparit State School, to Wesley College and then to the University of Melbourne, laden with scholarships, exhibitions and prizes. He was quickly successful at the Victorian Bar and few who knew him were surprised when he looked towards politics as a larger and more alluring arena for his talents. Touching thirty-four, he won an Upper House seat in the Victorian State Parliament in 1928.

His stay in the Victorian Upper House was brief. Great political careers are not made in such remote arenas. He resigned from the Council in 1929 to invade the Assembly and was the member for Nunawading until 1934. The ordinary mortals in the Victorian Legislative Assembly quickly understood that a presence was with them, brilliant, ambitious. They were an average and unexciting crowd of State parliamentarians. An exception was later to be an astonishing performer on the Victorian scene, plump Albert Dunstan, sometimes called the Billy Bunter of State politics. This was not a very apt description. He was as sly as, but far more dangerous than, the Owl of the Remove.

Unfortunately, Menzies did not have the opportunity to probe Dunstan's mind or to sample his talent for political intrigue. It would have been a valuable apprenticeship for Canberra. Leading the Labor Party in Victoria when Menzies swept in was a gangling farmer fondly known as Ned Hogan. Never had he seen inside Parliament anyone so glittering and witty as Menzies. When the member for Nunawading rose in his place to scourge and mock, Ned Hogan would swing round in his chair and settle back like a man in the front stalls to enjoy the show. He would gaze at Menzies with mouth agape, waiting for the moment to laugh. And then, right on the phrase, back would go his head and he roared with delight. Sir Stanley Argyle, Menzies' leader, was less appreciative. The newcomer was getting too many headlines. The brilliance of his young colleague was perhaps rather exhausting.

Who knows what Menzies expected to find in Canberra? Certainly not an Olympian club of intellectuals and wits. The Federal capital may have had the promise of things to come, but, by ordinary living standards, it was a bush town. And the Ministry assembled around that "perfect family man" Prime Minister Lyons was modest in its talents. It would be unkind to go through the whole list; pleasanter, indeed, to remember that Australia was still a little place. In Menzies' first year the Federal Government had a Budget of about £75 million. Australia had a High Commissioner in London and little else, diplomatically, anywhere in the world. "Those were days of noble simplicity," Menzies said thirty years later. One assumes he was talking about geography, architecture, and the problems of government, not about people in politics.

About this time Australia was coming out of the anguish and aftermath of depression. The people were busy about their own affairs and concerned about lining pockets empty for too long. Europe was far off. So was Hitler. How curious it is, looking back, to recall that men in Australia with access to the facts could not recognize Hitlerism for what it was. Menzies was not the only man in a key position to doubt those who saw in Hitler not only a threat to Europe but a menace to the whole world. Sir Keith Murdoch, one of the most powerful and influential of Australian newspaper proprietors, deplored the Cassandra-like warnings of Winston Churchill and his friends. Each time Hitler extended his boundaries the Murdochs of the time accepted the dictator's apologies and assurances that the limit of his ambitions had been reached. As the decade wore on, with portents terrible to those who could see, Canberra, like many other capitals, hoped for the best and did very little to prepare for the worst.

What did occupy the minds of the politicians in Canberra was the decay of the United Australia Party, which, from its creation, was rootless and artificial. If the U.A.P. was Australian, it was neither united nor a party in the sense the term is now understood. Led by a man from the Labor Party, the U.A.P. included politicians who had earlier paraded as members of the Nationalist Party. No effective party organization existed to discipline these individualists. In the Ministry the

8

polyglot character of the team was made more marked by the horse-traders of the Country Party. Looking back from now, the decline of the Lyons Government, reflected in the ballot box, was inevitable. The Government's backers had, in the first instance, not been motivated by positive political values but by a determination to bring down the Labor Government when it splintered under economic and financial pressures. In any normal set-up the sea-change of a lifelong Labor man into the leader of a conservative group would have been as incredible as the transformation of a member of the Melbourne Club from the Establishment to the Communist Party. But those who saw Australian politics as an exercise in keeping the Labor Party out of power thought that what had been done with Hughes could be done with Lyons.

This is not a political history: we move now to the decision by Menzies that led on to the first crisis of his political life. Who could have passed through it without being changed? How bitter, indeed savage, an interlude it was will not be revealed in the political memoirs of the period. When politicians in the autumn of their lives put down their meditations and their version of events we do not look for the ruthless honesty of Samuel Pepys. More predictable is the partisanship of a Saint-Simon. Presenting themselves in the most favourable light and reminiscing about unpleasant episodes, they forgive and forget, at least forget. All these evasions or personal reconstruction of events blur the passions and hates surrounding the last days of the Lyons Government and the events that immediately followed.

9

III

Bad News on Good Friday

THE ninth issue of the *Parliamentary Handbook* (1931 to 1938) has a section setting out "Ministries since the establishment of the Commonwealth." The pages devoted to the Lyons Ministry from 6th January 1932 record so many changes that one throws the book down, despairing of tracing the comings and goings of ministers. Conscious of this, the editors present a separate table of the Lyons Ministry as at 1st July 1938, together with the apology that "there have been numerous changes in the Ministry so that its present composition is not easily determined from the previous table." Then, to cap it, the patient researcher will come across an addendum saying that since the *Handbook* went to press Mr Lyons had formed a new Ministry on 7th November 1938. This table discloses Menzies third on the list after Lyons and Page. His portfolios are Attorney-General and Minister for Industry.

All this is not very enlightening; it is put down in the drab language of the *Handbook* as a reminder that the resignation of Menzies from the Lyons Ministry on 14th March 1939 was not unique. Other men had been cast out or had walked out. Long before Menzies resigned from the Ministry and from his position as deputy leader of the U.A.P. the smell of decay hung over the Government. The Lyons hailed as a saviour was now regarded as expendable by many who had enthroned him a few years earlier. His leadership was criticized. As the international situation grew more ominous Australia's defence programme looked hopelessly inadequate. Lyons himself fretted and worried. His health began to fail. Cabinet meetings were bitter and argumentative. There was an atmosphere of conspiracy and plotting. The struggle for power became naked.

Menzies has described Lyons as a great parliamentarian; he knew "every noise and every creak in the machinery, and he understands the human beings who are in Parliament. . . ." But the Lyons who performed so skilfully answering "Questions Without Notice" (he could disarm a malicious questioner with friendly and accommodating words that gave nothing away) was less adroit with the squabbling opportunists in his Cabinet.

In October 1938, some months before he resigned, Menzies addressed the Constitutional Association in Sydney. He spoke of the need for "inspiring leadership" in Australia. Such sentiments from a senior minister in the Government and the deputy leader of the U.A.P. were, not unnaturally, interpreted as an attack on Lyons, although the Prime Minister was not mentioned by name. Lyons offered no public comment. He tried to sustain the illusion of Cabinet solidarity. It was like trying to stop a flood. Many, many pages have been written by the chief actors and by observers off-stage about Menzies' resignation from the Lyons Ministry on 14th March 1939. The headline version was that the abandonment of National Insurance was the reason. Although this was mentioned by Menzies as a commitment from which he could not honourably escape, he said that "since last September I have more than once had the misfortune to find myself at variance with the majority of Cabinet on matters of moment, and in particular upon important aspects of our defence preparedness." He had refrained from resigning, he said, so that a common front might be preserved "at a period like this".

On the day Menzies walked out of the Government Hitler walked into Czechoslovakia. Most Australians who had followed the arrogant and menacing march of Hitler since his contemptuous repudiation of the Treaty of Versailles looked to London, Paris, Berlin and Moscow rather than to Canberra when the arguments began about Menzies' withdrawal to the back bench. Accusations of disloyalty were loud and bitter. But Menzies' stand on National Insurance, the angry denunciations of his most implacable opponent Earle Page, the mutterings of his other rivals for the leadership, and the final manoeuvres of the Prime Minister to prevent the complete collapse of his administration all were eclipsed when Lyons was struck down. Weary, perhaps desperate, the Prime Minister was in hospital in Sydney with a severe chill. A heart attack followed and on Good Friday Lyons was dead.

Observe the scene that now unfolds. The Prime Minister has died without disclosing to the Governor-General (Lord Gowrie) his views on the succession. The senior party in the coalition is without either a leader or a deputy leader. Earle Page, leader of the Country Party and Acting Prime Minister while Lyons was alive, calls a Cabinet meeting on the day of the Prime Minister's death. What is to be done? What is the constitutional procedure? In this dilemma the ministers turn to Hughes, Attorney-General in the place vacated by Menzies. He recommends that the Governor-General should be advised to commission Page to form a government. This course is followed, Lord Gowrie consents, and the leader of the Country Party becomes Prime Minister.

Sir Earle Page was Prime Minister of Australia from 7th April 1939 to 26th April 1939, not a long time, not a month. Time, however, is relative. The April days of 1939 for the men who hungered after the prime ministership were long days. The Earle Page who had assisted in the downfall of Hughes many years before, who had basked in the sunlight of Bruce's brief golden age and who had sat close to Lyons, was in the seat of power. It would be naïve to believe that he would merrily abandon it. To be a caretaker Prime Minister is like being a stand-in for a star. And Page did not have the temperament of a stand-in. He knew, of course, that his was the minority party. Carrying on with Lyons's Cabinet, he informed these gentlemen that he would relinquish his office when the U.A.P. chose a leader. So far the revelation was traditional. What followed was not. Page said that he would refuse to sit in Cabinet if Menzies were elected leader of the U.A.P. He had his own precedent for this declaration of war. In December 1922 Prime Minister Hughes had lost his slender majority in the House of Representatives and Earle Page's Country Party held the balance of power. Page exercised this power so uncompromisingly that all the Little Digger's twists and turns to find an accommodation were unavailing. Hughes was forced to a resignation and recommended Bruce, who, raised to power by Page, agreed to a coalition that lasted until the general election of 1929.

No doubt Page believed that, having overthrown so shrewd an adversary as Hughes, it would be much easier to stop Menzies. His resolve to do this was strengthened by his personal dislike. He was determined to defeat the man as well as the politician. It is possible that Menzies, still a novice in the technique of political skulduggery, had not made a close enough study of his enemy. Throughout its history the Country Party has attracted to its Federal parliamentary party men of tough fibre; tenacious men; hard fighters and unsentimental opportunists. The characteristics which their reluctant allies found least admirable in the Country Party were strong in Earle Page; for he beyond all others made, fashioned, and led the Country Party. He was wily, devious, persistent and, in his quarrels, implacable. The façade was deceptive. He acquired a hissing giggle to conceal his feelings and a verbal device—"Y'see, y'see, y'see"—as a substitute for argument. He cultivated obscurity as a weapon. He usually got what he wanted because he never gave up. Menzies may have been deceived in these early years by Page's external mannerisms. He was soon to learn how deadly Page's enmity could be.

But the Fates must not be scorned. Earle Page told the U.A.P. that he would accept any leader of their choosing except Menzies. He apparently believed that would be a potent enough veto to damn the man he disliked most in the race for leadership. His obsessional dislike set him upon a strange course. The reminiscences of the period suggest that Page, who had been Lyons's doctor as well as his friend, believed that Menzies had made even more intolerable the Prime Minister's burdens. There were other stories that nobody will ever be able to check. Menzies was a talented mimic. Around Canberra it was whispered that he had mimed Page in London. Who knows what the truth is? The fact of political life was that Page had resolved to do everything and more to obstruct, delay, defeat and for ever destroy Menzies' hopes of leadership. Into the period between 7th April 1939 and 26th April

13

1939, Page concentrated a fantastic amount of intrigue, and, finally, what can only be described as political madness, because when the battle ended Page was the defeated. In the brief space this king-maker was removed from the centre of the stage, not by those who were, like him, struggling for power, but by his own tribe.

IV

Bruce and the Spiders

An interlude now presented itself, a small comedy scene, although it was not designed as light entertainment by its creators. Newspapers solemnly recorded the affair. The principals did not imagine that later students of the politics of the 'thirties might find their conduct hilariously entertaining.

The affair took shape while Australians were still talking about the dead Prime Minister, the friendly, kindly, fatherly Labor exile from Tasmania. Obsequies cannot be permitted to interrupt political planning and plotting. So it was that certain gentlemen in Canberra decided that Menzies could be stopped before he got properly started if they could find and field a champion runner.

Page decided that Stanley Melbourne Bruce was the man. His ally in this extraordinary project was R. G. Casey, Treasurer in the Ministry of "the jolly old Doc". Surely only the bitter, frenzied nature of the situation could have set the wily Page on so strange a course. Bruce had served briefly under Lyons. He went to London in 1932 as Australian Minister, resigned his seat in the House of Representatives in 1933, and was appointed Australian High Commissioner in London. As Australia's man in London he was a nice choice. He was at home among the lordly. He had been in Australian politics from May 1918 and had not only seen his own government defeated but had been defeated himself at the general election of 1929, a humiliating experience for a Prime Minister. True, he had been re-elected to the House of Representatives in 1931, but Lyons was the hero, tolerated even by the Melbourne Establishment. All that unpleasantness was now behind Bruce, whose affection for Australia was deeper than his affection for Australian politics.

Bruce and Page had kept the marriage between their two parties reasonably harmonious for several years. As the husband in this marriage of convenience, Bruce knew how to handle a nagging wife. He usually let Page have his way because he discovered that Page got what he wanted anyhow. It was better to go quietly than be tormented by the doctor's persistence. But this time Page was not to get his way.

When the great idea burst upon Page's febrile mind Bruce was on his way back to England after a visit to Australia. The story goes that Page and Casey telephoned Bruce and offered him the world. He would be given a safe seat. He was needed. One can imagine Bruce's consternation. The story goes on that the urbane High Commissioner did not reject the passionate pleas out of hand but nominated impossible conditions. The essence was that he would be free to form a National Government with representatives of all parties. Either then or later Labor's John Curtin had indicated that his party would not join a National Government. Although strange things happen in politics, no sane student of affairs could have seen the Labor politicians who, with the help of Hughes, had destroyed Bruce, gladly raising him up again to national leadership. The feuds and factions of the Lyons administration would have been repeated more ferociously. The whole episode was crazy and came to nothing.

Page did not give up. By now it was common knowledge that Menzies would stand for the leadership of the U.A.P. Although he had many enemies, he had friends too. The lobbying was intense. Page's last defiance before the U.A.P. met to elect a leader was to threaten his coalition partners. The Parliamentary Country Party told the U.A.P. members by way of a resolution that it was "definitely unable" to co-operate in a government with Menzies as Prime Minister. Nor was it willing to give any undertaking to support a government led by Menzies.

Casey saw the end of the Bruce proposal when his own party met. They rejected the plan by deciding to proceed with the business of electing a leader and as the result was to show they declined to be intimidated by the angry Page.

V

Words Designed to Kill

FOUR members of the U.A.P. nominated for the leadership at the party meeting on 18th April 1939. Let us present them on this historic occasion in proper style: the Right Hon. Richard Gardiner Casey, the Right Hon. William Morris Hughes, the Right Hon. Robert Gordon Menzies, and the Hon. Thomas Walter White.

Three of the names are already familiar. The fourth contender requires a brief introduction. White had been in the House of Representatives since 1929 and Minister for Trade and Customs for about five years. He had left the Lyons Ministry in a most peculiar fashion. He walked out because he was sworn in the wrong order of precedence at Government House. If this hurt dignity provoked merriment in Canberra among the tough and the earthy, White never forgot he was a son-in-law of Alfred Deakin. Uncharitable Canberra professionals saw White as a pompous little man. They made fun of him without malice. Yet, before the political virus settled in him, he had been one of Australia's first to fly in war. The Turks captured him and he escaped by way of Russia. His adventures were recounted in his *Guests of the Unspeakable*, renamed "Jests of the Unspeakable" by the wits of the Labor Party. White ultimately found himself with a knighthood and with Australia House, London, as his setting as High Commissioner; he was not destined to be Prime Minister. What drives politicians to reach beyond their grasp is a subject for study by experts who peer into the mind of man. So the motives for White's decision to nominate remain inscrutable. He was not successful. White and Casey were eliminated first from the ballot. Menzies and Hughes were left to fight it out.

Now is the time to take a closer look at Hughes, for this astonishing personality meant business. He wanted the leadership. He wanted to be Prime Minister again and he had worked and organized intensely to beat Menzies. He was so old in years, experience, and political intrigue that he looked as ancient as a Pharoah and, indeed, might have walked out of Thebes to accost his big, hard, ambitious opponent. An ancient in 1939 he lived until 1952. He was tiny, wrinkled, and brown like a walnut, and survived his defeat in 1939 to lead the U.A.P. again. He was skin and bone. A strong breeze could have blown him away; a gale would not have drowned his voice. Walking through King's Hall or talking in the lounge of the Hotel Canberra, he was a spectacle for the visitor. But he was no museum piece to those at work in the business of politics. His sarcasm, invective, and wit gave colour if not light to Cabinet meetings.

Putting on his armour in April 1939 and lusting for battle, this waspish dyspeptic had entered the New South Wales Legislative Assembly in 1894 and he was then in his thirtieth year. Parkes was still in a House which had more talent (who can deny it?) than the Federal Parliament that saw the struggle for power in 1939. Hughes was a personality, a character, a politician trained in a hard and brilliant school before he walked into the House of Representatives in 1901. We had to wait more than a decade to see him brought to perfection as a national spectacle. World War I found him at the height of his powers. For years he had fought and provoked opponents to fury. Now he had an enemy to match his rage and will to win. He was utterly dedicated to the task of beating Germany and he was not pious about the means to the end. In those days he was swarthy, bony, black-eyed, fierce. He was so utterly single-minded that he split the Labor Party to beat the Kaiser. One peers into those faraway days to see processions ride by headed by a little man in a Digger hat carried by cheering giants in khaki. Low's inspired line has preserved that turbulent past in cartoons of extraordinary verve and wit. The original of one of the most inspired of those cartoons is now in Parliament House, Canberra. The setting is the Imperial Conference in 1916. Hughes has been introduced to Asquith's

18

Cabinet. The room is in chaos and Hughes is pounding the table. At the far end a nervous Asquith appeals to another wild Welshman, Lloyd George. And the caption says superbly: "David, talk to him in Welsh and pacify him!"

The war against Germany, and the Hall of Mirrors at Versailles, created the authentic Hughes. They defined what was best in him, a strength of mind that would not contemplate defeat. His mind was so much the master that it dominated, decade after decade, a tiny frame and a body tormented by dyspepsia. Early days of struggle and the stark battle to eat ruined his digestion. Thereafter he ate to live. Food was never a delight. There were times when he went for days without being able to take more than a morsel.

Is it surprising then that after World War I, after the Nationalists had taken the crown away from him, he should wander the political scene like a man without a home? He had become irritable and quarrelsome. There was no need to call a doctor. He was an exile from his party. He had broken with the Labor Party because he had a single-minded resolve to win the war. Nothing was allowed to stand in his way, not even a party that was intensely his own. He had planned and hoped to return to the A.L.P. after the war. The records tell the story. There was no place for him in a Labor Party led by a new generation. He was condemned to be a political exile.

After all the battles of the yesterdays, after campaigning in every election since Federation, first for West Sydney, then for Bendigo in Victoria, and back to New South Wales and North Sydney; after knowing ministerial office back to 1904; after all he had seen, plotted, and endured in politics he grasped at leadership and office again. He was hostile to Menzies partly because the big, ambitious younger man stood in his way and partly because he didn't like Menzies. "Menzies a leader!" he said in that high voice that could never sink to a whisper, "He couldn't lead a flock of homing pigeons!" But sarcasm, lobbying, and all the tricks Hughes knew did not win the leadership for him. After the votes were counted Menzies was leader of the U.A.P. and, as leader, the prime ministership was in his hands, almost.

Page still had his commission. The news that Menzies had won the U.A.P. leadership made him cling to his precarious office more obstinately. The brawling continued. Page angrily told Menzies, who formally called on him, that he would not serve in a Menzies Ministry and that his Country Party colleagues were of the same mind. "The feeling of my fellows is that they must take to the raft at once rather than sink in the same boat with him," he had informed Bruce.

Page, however, had resolved to bring on at once the disaster he prophesied and in the few hours before the end of this ugly chapter he disclosed his intentions to his party.

Although his friends and supporters in the Country Party had been trained in a hard school they were appalled. Emotional and unbalanced, the usually shrewd Page, normally an able and subtle tactician, had composed a speech which he was convinced would overthrow Menzies and strike down his leadership. The intention was to discredit Menzies personally, to cast doubt upon his judgement, his loyalty to his dead leader, and his courage. His shocked friends pleaded with Page to rewrite the speech. He would not accept their advice, nor appreciate that if he stood up in Parliament and uttered the words he had set down he would injure himself, not Menzies. What happened is now an unsavoury piece of political history. On 20th April, Page told the House of Representatives that he proposed immediately to resign the prime ministership. His bitter attack on Menzies followed. Nothing more offensive, more personal, more wounding had ever been heard in Federal Parliament.

Page's speech and Menzies' reply may be read in full in *Hansard*. Years later Page put down in his memoirs some words of atonement. But we are concerned here with the effect on Menzies of a cruel, unnecessary, and, indeed, futile attack. He was restrained in his reply in the House and members were sympathetic. Nobody could have carried it off with more poise and quality. So much for the surface. Underneath, he was deeply wounded. He was content to allow the people who knew and worked with him to make the judgement on his courage and capacity. That was the front he presented to Parliament and the nation. Yet this episode left its scar. Many years later when Menzies reached the high plateau of his career those who tried to understand and assess the man behind the political leader often forgot the scars of 1939. They were hidden behind the double-breasted suit. If sometimes the old wounds hurt who knew it when the Menzies of the late 'fifties and 'sixties rose in his place to be consciously brilliant?

VI

Farmers in a Frenzy

WITH blood, sweat and tears only a page or two away a respite is in order. Let us peep, for instruction, inside the Country Party room in Parliament House. Serious students of the art and science of politics may interpret more soberly the events summarized here. They were, indeed, significant and what flowed from them influenced our affairs. Described by scholarly writers as one-eyed, single-minded horse-traders the Country Party parliamentarians had to remove themselves from "the Doc." after his unpardonable personal attack on Menzies. His position as leader of the Country Party had become untenable. He survived until September 1939, bowing out in a contest that should have been illustrated by a William Hogarth. It would be over-simplifying the affair to say that Page manipulated his farmer colleagues like puppets, because there were ambitious as well as egotistical farmers in this band of brothers. Ambitious as Caesar and very able, John McEwen was one candidate for the leadership. He had arrived in Canberra the same year as Menzies and he had found his way into the Lyons Ministry. He had a dark and menacing appearance and came to be known as "Black Jack".

For who knows what reasons or prejudices the devious Doctor did not want McEwen to prevail. He was for a South Australian farmer who was to become perhaps Parliament's most colourful eccentric, a distinction requiring notable off-beat talents. Archie Galbraith Cameron could make as much uproar as all the clans in revolt. He looked like those dark, hairy Scots who once upon a time engaged in cutting English throats south of the border. He wore elastic-sided boots which he threw about in temper. He also had the curious habit of walking out of his boots and padding about Parliament in his socks. Full of sound and fury, he could be seen any time of the day or night discussing the defects, shortcomings and breeding of the whole tribe of politicians. Into Cameron's eager hands Page thrust the party leadership after a party room vote that might easily· have been conducted in a lunatic asylum. Neither Cameron nor McEwen chose to vote and, for good measure, we have it on the authority of the Country Party's historian that four of the Country Party parliamentarians were debarred from voting.

Cameron was leader of the Country Party at the time of the sour September 1940 general election. Reduced in its numbers the party looked again at its leadership. This was insufferable to the haughty Cameron. He declined to put his position to the test, stood aloof, would not vote in a ballot for his successor. His tough, rustic colleagues ignored his Highland fury and went on with the rugged business of picking a leader. The incensed but rejected Cameron left the Country Party and resigned from the Ministry. His individualism became more conspicuous, his denunciations more comprehensive. He was ultimately silenced by his elevation to the Speaker's chair. Wigged and enthroned, he looked like a 1715 Jacobite.

Indifferent to the outraged pride of the Highlander, the hard-bargaining farmers went to work. Page was in the lists again. Why not? In politics are not all things forgiven and forgotten, y'see, y'see? But McEwen had not forgotten.

If Page was the White Champion, McEwen was the Black Knight. They jousted and the lances split. Each was awarded eight votes in the ballot. The partisans stood their ground. At this point Page was inspired. Implacable as ever, he hit upon the compromise that would deny McEwen and find a leader. Suddenly the mantle over which they had wrangled fell on the unsuspecting shoulders of the member for Darling Downs. Arthur Fadden was a newcomer. He had reached Canberra by way of a by-election in 1936. He had no obvious ambitions and he suffered from no delusions of grandeur. He was amiable and gregarious. On that crazy day and in that turbulent room the Country Party elected Fadden as deputy leader with the status of leader. If this meant that when the clouds rolled by either rosy-cheeked Page or black-browed McEwen would

23

take his destined place, the opportunists were to be confounded. Fadden stayed at the top, perhaps because even the Canberra farmers were tired of Page's twists and turns, Cameron's elastic-sided boots, and McEwen's ambitions. By contrast Fadden had an enormous sense of fun, a zest for living, the gift of friendship. Produced like a rabbit out of a hat as a compromise, he survived the madness of the times to become, briefly, a Prime Minister and for many years one of the architects of an enduring coalition.

VII

Raised Up and Cast Down

HAVING reached the top more experienced as an inhabitant of the jungle, Menzies selected his team and gazed from his eminence upon a darkening world. He had been raised up. He was perhaps too young in the ways of politics to fear that he might be cast down. He had suffered one ordeal; he did not know he was to pass through another more devastating than the first. Pride goeth before a fall could be the text for what was to happen. However one describes it, there was a nice quality of medievalism about the next ordeal.

The first Menzies Ministry was all U.A.P.* It had to be. The names tell a story. He had to include some who had resisted his advance to the prime ministership. He also brought in friends and supporters. Senator McBride was there, Pickwickian Senator George McLeay, Eric Harrison, and a young man who brought up the rear, Harold Holt. He had entered Parliament at a by-election in 1935. Three members of this first Menzies Ministry were marked down for death. A U.A.P. divided and weak was to lose in a plane crash Air Minister Fairbairn, Army Minister Street, and Sir Henry Gullett. This disaster was a tragic prelude to melancholy events.

Colossal tasks confronted the new Government. No apologist could say that it was well-equipped. Years of attrition under Lyons, the brutal struggle for power after his death, the feuding inside the decaying U.A.P., and the quarrel with the Country Party, were a dark background against which to

* *Menzies Ministry*, from 26th April 1939 to 14th March 1940: R. G. Menzies, W. M. Hughes, R. G. Casey, G. A. Street, H. S. Gullett, G. McLeay, H. S. Foll, E. J. Harrison, J. N. Lawson, F. H. Stewart, J. V. Fairbairn, J. A. Perkins, P. C. Spender, P. A. McBride, H. B. Collett, H. E. Holt.

C

build a government and a party strong enough to meet the challenges of the day. Australia now knew that war was inevitable. No longer did sensible observers of the world scene argue about Hitler's intentions. The only question was when and where he would strike.

One or two other political facts should be put down here. Five months after Menzies selected his one-party Ministry war was declared. In March 1940 Menzies reconstructed his Cabinet to include five members of the Country Party. By this time Page had lost the Country Party leadership and he was not one of the five who formed the Ministry. In September 1940, a black period of the war in Europe, the Federal election in Australia disclosed an increasing loss of public confidence in both the U.A.P. and the Country Party. U.A.P. members shrank from twenty-five to twenty-two. The Country Party declined from sixteen to thirteen. In short, the balance of power in the Parliament of a country engaged in war was held by two Victorian Independents, Mallee wheat farmer Wilson and Arthur Coles of the well-known business family. In the Ministry selected by Menzies after the electoral reverse of September, Arthur Fadden went up to be Treasurer and Page came back to be Minister for Commerce. The Prime Minister knew that life would be hard; he did not realize how hard.

A whole book, perhaps a shelf of books, could be written about the Commonwealth's twenty-second Ministry, the Menzies Ministry born on 28th October 1940, dying on 29th August, 1941.

It covers an important period in Australia's war history and an intensely interesting political chapter. The detailed study is for the historians. We are concerned here with the effect on Menzies' personality of the campaign that led to his resignation. Perhaps no leader with so precarious a majority in Parliament in time of war could have survived for long. But Menzies had more to contend with than a critical electorate and an increasingly critical Press. His opponents, not the political opponents on the Opposition benches, but those on his own side of politics, were ready to spring on him and pull him down. The opportunity for an organized

26

campaign to discredit him as a leader presented itself early in 1941 when Menzies left Australia to visit Britain and theatres of war in which Australian troops were engaged. Those who joined in the campaign were not all his personal enemies. Some believed that he was not a war-time administrator. Others said that his gift of speech was not matched by the flair for action. Again, it was said that he was not a leader of men, that the breed of politicians needed a leader with a heart as well as a head. Closer to the seat of power were men who bitterly resented his hard mind, his arrogance, his refusal to court the crowd, his caustic tongue, his ambition. Finally, he was not the head of a political party with roots deep in the electorates, with a nation-wide organization, with a non-parliamentary leadership to exercise restraints on the Canberra politicians. Menzies, indeed, was the leader of a parliamentary party in an advanced state of dissolution. But this historical fact did not make any more palatable the methods used to bring him down before the destroyers managed also to bury the U.A.P.

Churchill was in command and the bombs were falling on England when Menzies arrived. Although he was no stranger, this England under fire was strange. He walked the blazing streets. He saw what was coming from the skies and saw how England took it all. He talked in the Menzies manner and there were Englishmen who said he was superb. The newspapers praised him. He came to know Churchill intimately. On his way back he visited Canada and the United States. He was received with the utmost cordiality. The return to Australia may not have been a triumphal procession, but the people wanted to hear him. They were impatient for leadership. Shortly after his return he addressed a huge meeting in Sydney and his topic was defined as "a blueprint for a total war effort". Then the Prime Minister went back to Canberra to talk to the House of Representatives.

In the harvest years of his prime ministership Menzies acquired fine skills as a professional. He learned, as the accomplished actor learns, that he must superbly control himself and discipline himself to control an audience. The House of Representatives is always a difficult audience, but Menzies knew, later, how to catch it, how (when he wanted to) he could impress the professionals. In 1941 he was a polished speaker but not as commanding as in later years. He was also addressing an Opposition that could smell the decay on the Government side and behind him, as he spoke, were men even then planning his downfall. He was fresh from the tremendous experience of London ablaze. He had returned from the theatres of war to the stage of party politics, a transition that exacerbated him. For him, for those who supported him, and for those who worked ceaselessly to overthrow him, the next few weeks were pretty sordid. Politics is rarely an activity that brings out the most civilized qualities in men; it is incredibly squalid when the knives are out.

The combination of forces against Menzies was overwhelming. So vast was the array that those who wanted him to go, either because they disliked him or because they believed he could not lead, might have arranged the exit in the traditional, good-mannered style. The final moves had to be made by the politicians. Most of them emerge from the episode as little men. They appear in this guise because of their methods. Political assassination is a well-known technique. Usually the victim is removed neatly and with appropriate expressions of regret on all sides. Often he finds himself numbered among the knights of the realm. Or he is translated to diplomacy and gracefully takes an ambassadorship. On other occasions ministers employ the stylish method of resignation, composing long epistles to their leader, who, in turn, replies with equally long letters in the mode of Lord Chesterfield. The men who had prayed and worked for the fall of Menzies were not so delicate. His opponents simply forced his resignation. Those who felt they could no longer serve under him did not hand in their portfolios, which, theoretically, would have given him the opportunity to approach others. Even at the U.A.P. meeting on the day of his resignation no vote was taken on the leadership. In short, Menzies' enemies got rid of him in the most brutal and undignified way imaginable.

A few days before the end a curious proposal was put to Parliament. On the surface it had no connection with the plans of the head-hunters. Indeed, Menzies himself told the

House of Representatives what was in mind. On 20th August 1941 he spoke briefly on the war situation and then said: "My colleagues in the Cabinet have, as a result of recent discussions, asked me to pay another visit to London. Having regard to the balance of parties in Parliament, I have indicated that it would not be practicable for me to go abroad at present, except with the approval of all parties. . . ."

Less than three months had elapsed since his return to Australia. But sudden changes and developments had happened on the battlefields. Germany had invaded Russia, Japan had occupied French Indo-China. "It is of great importance," Menzies said, "that Australia's voice should be directly heard in the place in which the major decisions are inevitably made." That place was Britain's War Cabinet.

Labor Opposition Leader Curtin replied to the Prime Minister twenty-four hours later. He announced the Labor Party's decision: "Having regard to the gravity of the war as it affects the Commonwealth, it is essential for Australia to have its Prime Minister here to direct the administration in the organization of a total war effort." Somebody else would have to speak for Australia in London.

Hughes stood up when Curtin sat down and passionately defended the projected mission. At this time, he said, London was the only place from which Australia could be guided. And Menzies was the man to speak for Australia. There could be no adequate substitute. On and on went Hughes, the eloquent defender of his leader!

Once Curtin had spoken the proposal was doomed and the Government would have ended the debate had it been sure of the numbers. A somewhat different colour was given to the proceedings when F. M. Forde, the Labor member for Capricornia, began by saying that if one could take notice of rumours the Attorney-General's speech was "not altogether disinterested".

"The people should be told the whole story of the political manoeuvring to get rid of the Prime Minister," Forde went on. "Members of the Government want to send him to London, not because they consider him to be the best man to represent Australia, but because some of them believe that they ought to occupy the post of Prime Minister, and each of them is angling to have Mr Menzies out of the way so that he may be displaced from office here."

That was on 21st August. A week later Menzies ceased to be Prime Minister. The cynics said that Hughes seven days earlier had discovered great virtues in Menzies only to get him out of the way. Forde's words may not have been attuned to the mood Hughes tried to create in the House, but the historian is likely to find them near to the truth.

One does not require exceptional interpretive gifts to recognize the anguish and bitter disappointment behind the Prime Minister's public announcement of his resignation "A frank discussion with my colleagues in the Cabinet has shown that while they have personal goodwill towards me many of them feel that I am unpopular with large sections of the press and people, and that this unpopularity handicaps the effectiveness of the Government by giving rise to misrepresentation and misunderstanding of its activities, and that there are divisions of opinion in the Government parties themselves which would not or might not exist under another leader. . . ."

Late on the night of 28th August 1941, the joint U.A.P.-Country Party meeting was as turbulent as a Praetorian Guard. Disposing of one leader, it confirmed another almost simultaneously. Having cut off its own head, the U.A.P. could not find another in its own disorganized ranks. It conferred the purple on the relatively new Country Party leader. On that strange night Arthur Fadden was designated Prime Minister and was sworn in the following day.

Many of the participants have written their version of this affair. One or two have tried to snatch a little glory from an event creditable to nobody. Political assessments have been made although it may yet be too early for final political judgements. Here we do no more than look as closely as we may upon a man who was rejected and humiliated. Not many in Australia at the end of August 1941 would have given tuppence for the political future of Robert Gordon Menzies. He was down and his enemies and his critics thought cheerfully that he was out.

Fadden carried on as Prime Minister from 29th August to

7th October 1941, with Menzies' ministers. Menzies himself was there, described as Minister for Defence Co-ordination. Nothing had been changed except the leader. Citizens did not joyfully rush into the streets to shout and cheer. If it is true that they had lost confidence in Menzies, they had not found confidence in Fadden, who was relatively unknown in those days. Canberra, of course, knew him as a droll character with an enormous zest for living, a tough constitution, and a large capacity for work and play. Some of the politicians may sincerely have believed that Fadden's earthy friendliness was the cure they were seeking. If so, they deluded themselves. The coalition needed more than a heart transplant. Unlamented by the electors, the Fadden Government was slain by the votes of Independents Coles and Wilson on a censure by the Labor Party and John Curtin became Prime Minister of Australia.*

"So I had a meeting of my party," laconically said Menzies many years later. It is indeed bewildering to trace the crazy pattern of those Canberra events of 1941. Although Menzies had been forced out of the Prime Minister's office, his leadership of the U.A.P. had not been challenged. And so, when the Fadden Government fell, Menzies called his party together. Fadden had been defeated on the floor of Parliament. The U.A.P. and the Country Party were now in Opposition and the U.A.P. was numerically the larger of the two parties. One assumed that the larger party would find an Opposition leader. Menzies obviously expected this. He had still much to learn. Up rose honourable gentlemen and spoke thus: "True, we are the larger party in Opposition, but, you know,

* Here is an extract from *Hansard* of October 3, 1941:
Mr Coles (Henty)—For some time I have been deeply concerned over conditions prevailing in this chamber, and I assume that today honourable members are not debating the budget, whatever good or bad points it may contain. We are debating a proposal which is really a motion of want of confidence in the ability of the Government to carry on. . . . I told the Prime Minister that I would vote against this Government today because he cannot give any assurance to the Parliament. I contend that he gave to the Governor-General an assurance which he was not justified in giving, because he had not then consulted me. I told those Ministers who approached me when the ex-Prime Minister was being removed, that I would not stand for it, and that I would not support the Government. . . .

we think you ought not to be Leader of the Opposition."
Their actual words may have been harsher. At this point
Menzies signed off. He rose on those large feet, gazed upon his
colleagues, and told them that a party unwilling to lead was
not worth leading. Having propounded a view he believed
politically important—"a party that is unwilling to lead is not
worth leading"—he resigned the leadership of the U.A.P. and
from late in 1941 until the great Curtin electoral victory in
1943 he sat in the Opposition corner of the House of Representatives. He sat there and waited.

Who took his place as leader of the U.A.P.? The obvious
guess is right. They selected Hughes, the ancient exile from
the Labor Party. Hughes, of course, was delighted. He would
never be Prime Minister again, but he was sitting on top of
the U.A.P. And he was determined to remain on top. He hit
upon an excellent device. Elected leader by a meeting of the
party, he could be discharged from his office only by another
meeting. So what could be simpler than not to have party
meetings? As the months went by and as his colleagues, at first
bewildered, became impatient and then angry, Hughes was
deaf—what a word!—to all requests for a meeting. Only an
electoral disaster for the U.A.P. that gave the Labor Party six
years of power broke the little man's resistance. It was high
comedy except for the victims of his cranky, authoritarian
rule.

Part Two

THE RENASCENCE

I

The Slaughter of 1943

RETIRING to a back-bench in the Opposition corner of the House, Robert Gordon Menzies had time to reflect on a period of 856 days as Prime Minister. It had been an experience in human relations unusual even in the rugged uplands of Australian politics. What was its effect on Menzies, seen by observers of the political game as a man with an ox-like constitution, a massive and resilient physical presence, a vast ambition, and a first-rate mind? If they were the sum of his qualities, the answer might be that he had been mauled but could await a new opportunity, a second chance. Superficially, some of his supporters may have felt that way.

After the fall he looked no different outwardly. He was to be seen striding buoyantly about Canberra, his cheeks ruddy, his eyes bright. He was a prized guest at dinner parties, an urbane and witty companion at the cocktail hour. Sometimes he appeared deceptively as the brilliant man who had reached the high point of his political career, savoured the office, and then contemptuously rejected a stage on which fools had to be tolerated. He graced a scene he had once dominated. "He is young," they said over the cocktails. "He is an able lawyer. Politics is not quite his field. Why does he stay on?"

Behind the urbane façade was another Menzies. Even those who stood by him had much to learn; his enemies were astonishingly astray in their assessments. The belief that he would not stand up and fight was widespread and ill-founded, as was the opinion that he could be destroyed by a body-blow. He was damned as arrogant, superior, and supremely selfish. His excessive sensitivity was not recognized only because it was concealed. His intuitions were not perceived by men less intuitive. The great miscalculation was that Menzies was strong in conceit but weak in staying power. The future was to disclose a prodigious stamina, an acute sensitivity, and a determination as big as his frame. In the months following his defeat he not only resolved to make a come-back; he would not only return; he would make his enemies eat their words. After 1941 he had another objective—to be at the top and to be invulnerable.

Those who relished his temporary absence from the centre of affairs should have studied Menzies' feet as closely as they watched the tilt of his head. Feet-watching may be as instructive as hand-reading. The Menzies bulk demanded strong legs and feet, but those feet often gave away what was hidden behind closed lips. In later years, in the period of his unchallenged rule, it was a revelation to walk behind Menzies as he mounted a flight of stairs. Slowly and purposefully the feet rose and fell upon each succeeding stair. The ground shook slightly. Each foot met the stair firmly, flatly, and authoritatively. He moved upward more like a force than a person. One had the feeling that anything or anybody in his way would be trodden down.

However, back in 1941, nobody bothered to study the ex-Prime Minister's feet.

One afternoon during this back-bencher interlude the members of the U.A.P. straggled into the House of Representatives after the bells had ceased ringing. It was obvious that they had just emerged from a protracted party meeting which, in turn, suggested to the initiated that it had been an angry meeting. What they wrangled about doesn't matter; Menzies' demeanour was far more significant. One could see his big frame from any part of the House or galleries. On this occasion the big face, from hairline to neckline, was a study in scarlet.

In one of his delicious essays Max Beerbohm tells how two gentlemen hiding in a tree in Windsor Park watched George the Fourth in his last days taking his morning drive far from inquisitive eyes. His face, they saw, was like a great, fiery sunset. That afternoon in the House of Representatives the face of Menzies was like a sunset, and, like a sunset, the colour ebbed slowly. It seemed a very long time before the normal colouring returned. Few in the galleries observed the spectacle. Those who did knew infallibly that underneath that calm exterior were forces of volcanic intensity.

In the House of Representatives on 8th October 1941 certain formalities took place after Mr Speaker Nairn read prayers. On this occasion John Curtin sat at the table at the right of the Speaker's Chair. "I formally announce," he said, "that on October 3 consequent upon the carrying of an amendment moved by me in the Committee of Supply, the Honourable A. W. Fadden submitted the resignation of his Government to His Excellency the Governor-General. Subsequently His Excellency commissioned me to form a ministry, which was sworn in on October 7."

Thus began a period of Labor rule enduring until 1949.

Two other formal announcements were made on the afternoon of 8th October. Fadden told the House that he had been unanimously appointed leader of the Opposition by a joint meeting of the United Australia Party and Country Party; and Hughes stood up to say that he had been elected leader of the United Australia Party.

Nobody mentioned Robert Gordon Menzies. From that afternoon until after the Federal election of 1943 he sat as a back-bencher. Only on the adjournment of the House on 8th October 1941 was any reference made to the fantastic events leading to the commissioning of the Curtin Ministry. A Labor Party elder statesman, Frank Brennan, philosophized about the role of government. He said that proposals for a national government, heard from the U.A.P. after the September 1940 election, would have been a fraud upon the electorate. He also said that "the overthrow of the head of the Menzies Government was a piece of unconscionable head-hunting which gained for the succeeding Government the

ridicule of the country and the political contempt of honourable members on this side of the chamber."

On that reflective note the House of Representatives
adjourned and a new Prime Minister who had been a life-long
pacifist found himself in the role of war leader of a country
soon to be threatened by the invasion of its shores. His
Treasurer and right-hand man was J. B. Chifley.

In a reminiscent mood many years later Menzies said that
Curtin and Chifley would never be understood until it was
realized that they were utterly different. "I have never known
two men more unlike," he said. "They were great friends but
two men more unlike I would never expect to see." This was
correct. Curtin and Chifley were dissimilar both in temperament and in outlook. Curtin's mind was far-ranging and
philosophical; Chifley's was concentrated on financial and
economic problems and he was more a pragmatist than a
philosopher.

In those critical days of war, however, the nation looked
to John Curtin and witnessed a strange transformation.

He became one of the finest of the Labor Party's Federal
leaders, yet he was an unusual man for the role; indeed, a
strange type. Before he went into Federal Parliament in 1928
he had been a newspaperman and a trade union official. These
descriptions tell us little. He had been a heavy drinker. Who
knows why, because when responsibility was thrust heavily
upon him he never drank again. He continued to smoke with
nervous intensity, but he put the bottle away. He was shy
and aloof when Canberra knew him well. Close friends were
few; the job was almost everything. He took over from Scullin
as leader of the Federal Labor Party in October 1935, an
unexpected choice, what they called "a clean-skin". Overnight,
this shy and sensitive M.P. from Fremantle became Federal
leader of a party with a turbulent history. Could he lead?
Could he dominate Caucus?

If you knew him well and if you had occasion to talk with
him, he might put his feet up on the table and talk about books
and poetry and history. Politics in the narrow sense was the
last thing he wanted to talk about. Quickly, however, Parliament saw in him a man of quality with a fine command of

language. On great occasions he could bind the House with his words. He had integrity. As a nation's leader in critical years of war, this man to whom warfare was abhorrent found in himself reserves of courage to sustain him in the making and the carrying out of decisions imperative for the nation and critical for his own party. One of his most compelling speeches in Parliament, short but carrying with it a high sense of history, announced the joining of the Battle of the Coral Sea with all its impact on the safety of Australia. Later, this Labor leader who had become the leader of a nation won a reluctant Labor Party to support his conscription legislation, for his Militia Bill was precisely that. The enormous responsibilities he carried killed him before the war against Japan ended, but this great Australian, a pacifist and a socialist, acquired the talents of a strategist and the assurance to oppose a Churchill.

The impact Curtin made on the Australian people was spectacularly seen in the Federal election of 1943. True, fears that the Japanese would invade Australia had been replaced by a sober conviction that American power, enormously deployed, would ultimately defeat the Japanese militarists. On the European battlefields the signs were that Hitler, no matter how savagely he persisted, would fail in the end. It was in this changing atmosphere that Curtin led a now united Labor Party to the polls. He had deeply impressed Parliament by his quality and leadership; the campaign was to show that the nation also believed in him.

Fadden, as leader of the Opposition, was awakened from sleep the night he delivered his policy speech, to be told by a newspaperman that Menzies had rejected an important item in his programme. Testily Fadden described this as another stab in the back. Later he was to say that Menzies' statement was fatal to the concept of a United Opposition. But who could honestly say there was unity in the men led by Fadden? For some time Menzies had been the leader of a group within the U.A.P. that called itself the National Service Group. The obstinate refusal of Hughes to call party meetings inevitably led to the unofficial group around Menzies. Angrily, Hughes had written a pamphlet denouncing the rebels, a bitter piece of writing that described Menzies as "helpless as a beetle on its back". To all insiders and most outsiders the Opposition was not united. That, however, was not a critical factor in the 1943 election. It is an axiom of politics that oppositions are not elected; governments are either confirmed in office or rejected. The most surprising feature of the 1943 election was the completeness of the confirmation.

For Curtin the election campaign was like a Roman triumph. Half-way through the campaign, at a tremendous public meeting in Melbourne, the crowd roared its approval, cheered, stamped, and thundered its ovation. After the meeting, while Curtin stood in the body of the hall surrounded by friends, an elderly stranger pressed forward, grasped one of the Prime Minister's hands and enthusiastically kissed it. Curtin drew his hand back as though it had been bitten. He was acutely embarrassed.

In Adelaide the reception was wilder. Almost from the beginning to the end of the meeting an animal roar of approval was heard. One did not have to be an expert in campaigning to smell a Labor victory.

On the day before the vote Fadden ended his tour in Sydney. He walked into the foyer of the Hotel Australia carrying his bags. He was pale and tired. And he was alone. On the Saturday night he and the rest of Australia saw the figures go up that announced a sweeping Labor Party victory and a final and devastating defeat for the U.A.P. and the Country Party. Menzies saw it all too.

"We had been almost butchered," he said in later years. "Our side of politics had the biggest thrashing it ever had." The battered remnant of the U.A.P. went back to Canberra despised and rejected and still led by the fabulously ancient Hughes whose political life was regarded as finished by most people. In this climate of defeat, cold as ice, the survivors looked at one another—and then most of them looked at Menzies. In retreat from the littered battlefield they asked him if he would care to be leader!

This is how he replied: "Yes, but I must be leader of the Opposition which was denied me in 1941, and above all I must have the right, the clear right, to develop a new party." They bowed to this; and so, in September 1943, Menzies again became leader of the U.A.P. The years of his exile had taught him that the ambitions of individuals could not lead on to power and office unless men were united; that one guarantee of unity was a strongly based political organization, lucid in its political beliefs, firm in its principles, and forward-looking in its programme. More than anything, however, political unity was imperative. The task he set himself was to plan and create this marvel; for in the atmosphere of September 1943 what he thought of seemed utterly beyond attainment.

II

Dark Hours Before Dawn

THE news of Curtin's 1943 triumph brought forth no loud lamentations from the Australian community. Overwhelmingly the electors had voted for the Government, and that was that. A hard core of conservatives,* however, had anticipated the disintegration of the U.A.P. As early as April 1943 the Liberal Democratic Party was launched in New South Wales by angry men who really believed that Australia might fall to the socialists and the communists. The promoters of the Liberal Democratic Party described themselves as spokesmen for "the little people who have so far been inarticulate". About this time disillusioned U.A.P. supporters organized the Commonwealth Party, also dedicated to the defeat of Labor.

Too late even to survive, the lay backers of the U.A.P. in New South Wales talked about reorganization. A dying impulse to form a national party faded when moves to confer with the U.A.P. in Victoria came to nothing.

By November 1943 the conservative forces in New South Wales had fragmented. Influential citizens from the Institute of Public Affairs convened a conference of representatives of the U.A.P., the Liberal Democratic Party, the Commonwealth Party, and the Country Party. Unity was the treasure they sought. The Country Party delegates vanished after a few hours. As they fled they told the others that their Constitution pre-

* Some observers of the Australian political scene use "conservative" as a general term applicable to supporters of the old Nationalist Party, the U.A.P., and the Liberal Party. Others employ the negative term "non-Labor". One of the minor mysteries of politics in Australia has been the readiness of members of the parties in question to describe themselves as "non-Labor". A cynical explanation may be that before the Liberal Party of Australia was formed "non-Labor" was an apt description.

vented them from helping to form a new party. Those who remained found unanimity in their opposition to "the socialistic forces of the Labor Party" and agreed that "unity of all organizations opposed to socialism" was imperative. These negative discoveries were a poor basis for a new party. Nevertheless, the council of the New South Wales U.A.P. decided to dissolve its organization and seek a brave new world with the Commonwealth and Liberal Democratic Parties.

The sequel was sad. A "political philosophy" is not written when men stand up calling for three cheers for Private Enterprise and Individual Freedom and three hearty hoots for the Labor Party. The urge behind these men was to defeat the Labor Party rather than to think and act positively in the formulation of alternative programmes and policies. Most of them were amateurs in a hurry and the others were U.A.P. professionals who at least knew something about political organizations. There was no commanding personality among them, no man of national repute. Angry, parochial, and inexperienced, they failed to discover a political unity for their own State. So they made little impact across the borders.

The situation in Victoria was no less messy. The United Australia Party in that State was a many-headed monster. One head spoke for the United Australia Organization, another for the Australian Women's National League, another for the Young Nationalists' Organization, another for the National Union. This frightening spectacle helped to produce the Services and Citizens Party and the Middle Class Organization.

In every State except South Australia the conservatives were fragmented and frustrated. In South Australia the Liberal and Country League, preserving a splendid coalition, was the effective voice of conservatism and was ably led by Thomas Playford.

The death agonies of the U.A.P. and the activities of those who tried either to revive the corpse or stand in its place did not excite the multitude. Death and violence of a large order were in the headlines, for the outcome of the world at war was still unknown. In this situation the citizenry cared little about the doings of political organizations popping up like mush-

41

D

rooms. Among those who joined this crop of parties were men angered by the prospect of a Labor Government in the days of peace to come ruling with the far-ranging powers surrendered to it in the emergency of war. Others felt strongly that they must have a political organization to speak for them. In Canberra, however, Prime Minister Curtin, caught up in the ugly business of war, had little time to make plans for a Socialist Australia.

The pattern changed in 1944. Strikes which the Labor Government was unable to control resulted in loss of production and inconvenience for the public. Transport stoppages and meatless weekends irritated suburbia. "We are confronted by industrial anarchy," thundered the leader-writers.

Arthur Calwell, Labor's Minister for News and Information, collided with the Sydney Press on the issue of political censorship. Editions were seized. The High Court was invoked and upheld the view of the newspapers that they were not necessarily breaching security censorship when they criticized the Government for imposing a political censorship.

August 1944 was a key month politically. Long before this Herbert Vere Evatt had been a significant figure in the Labor hierarchy; but now he was in a blaze of light. As Attorney-General he devised the "Fourteen Powers" Referendum. It was proposed by this measure to insert a new section (60A) in the Constitution, empowering the Commonwealth, for a period of five years after the end of the war, to legislate on employment, marketing, the production and distribution of foods, and other aspects of Australian life. Constitutional guarantees of freedom of speech and religion and safeguards against the abuse of delegated legislative power were promised. But the electors could not pick and choose from this mixed bag. They were required to vote for the proposed alterations as a whole.

This was a challenge to the bickering groups trying to form a front against the Labor Party. Evatt was presented as a sinister figure concocting a plot to take over Australia in the name of socialism. Arguments that transitional powers were needed to ease Australia from a wartime to a peacetime economy did not impress electors who traditionally refused to increase the powers of the central government.

Menzies was out campaigning and his political nose picked up the scent. The strength of public opinion against the Powers Referendum encouraged him to take the decisive steps leading to the formation of a new party. All over the country people told him that he would have their votes if he could offer them a united party. On 19th August 1944 the electorate which had enthusiastically voted for the Curtin Government at the general election of late 1943 rejected the referendum. The proposed constitutional alteration had been sugared with the label of "Post-war Reconstruction and Democratic Rights", but the verdict of the voters was that they would be reconstructed on less arbitrary lines than Evatt had planned for them. A touch of colour came to the cheeks of Labor's opponents. Menzies sensed that the time to act had come. He told his parliamentary colleagues that he would call a conference to discuss the establishment of a national political movement. In the jargon of politics he told his willing listeners that the referendum campaign showed clearly that a great body of public opinion "is not prepared to accept socialism as the pathway to human happiness".

For months Menzies had been planning and working. He knew from bitter experience that he would never again become Prime Minister unless he could build on the foundations of a nationwide political organization, with the support of the rank-and-file troops as well as officers, with party unity, national policy and a national platform. His determination was such that he was not dismayed by all the sound and fury of the bickering groups in Sydney and Melbourne.

Early in September 1944 Menzies sent a famous letter to the various organizations that were ineffectually seeking the way to a promised land of unity. This letter was the beginning of so much that it deserves reprinting in full:

> The time seems opportune for an effort to secure unity of action and organization among those political groups which stand for a liberal, progressive policy and are opposed to socialism with its bureaucratic administration and restriction of personal freedom.
> The Australian Labor Party has an efficient Commonwealth-wide organization. To resist effectively those aspects

of Labor policy to which we are opposed and to gain the public support enabling governments sympathetic to our views to be formed we must match Labor's organization with an Australian organization of our own. This organization should possess an Australian policy and have the closest contact with its parliamentary leaders and representatives.

I therefore invite you to be present at a conference to be held at Canberra on October 13th, 14th and 16th.

I sincerely hope that you will participate in a full and frank discussion. You will be entirely free to make your own decisions and will not, of course, be bound by any majority of other persons.

It is possible that a further conference will be found necessary after our first discussion has taken place, but my colleagues and I believe it to be most desirable that those of us who share the same broad political beliefs should first see if a basis can be found for unity.

A successful outcome of such discussion might quickly and completely alter the current of Australian politics.

III

The Canberra and Albury Miracles

THE leaderless legion assembled at the squat little Masonic Hall not far from Parliament House. The setting was not glamorous. Trestle tables and hard seats, not banners and bands, greeted the delegates when the conference was opened at three o'clock on the afternoon of 13th October. The portents were not auspicious.

Including Menzies, the Federal parliamentary delegation numbered twelve. Loyal Eric Harrison was present as deputy leader of the Opposition, and among the faithful were tubby Senator McLeay and Senator Leckie.

Politicians from the States included R. W. D. Weaver, leader of the Opposition in New South Wales; T. T. Hollway who led the U.A.P. in Victoria; and Premier Playford of South Australia, who, apart from Menzies, was perhaps the only one present known across the Continent.

Eleven women sat among the delegates. The most formidable of them came from the Australian Women's National League in Victoria. Their president was the strong-minded Mrs Claude Couchman who had the air of a duchess and a voice of command.

The rest were a mixed bag. They came from the Institute of Public Affairs, the Australian Constitutional League, the Democratic Party, the Liberal Democratic Party, the Liberal and Country League of South Australia, the Country-National Organization of Queensland, the Victorian United Australia Organization, the Nationalist Party in Victoria, the Services and Citizens Party, and there were even two observers from the Kooyong Citizens' Association.

There were eighty delegates or observers representing eighteen organizations. A few of them were later to rise to the top of the Liberal Party Organization. W. H. Anderson from the Services and Citizens Party was a delegate; he was to become a distinguished Federal President of the party. Another future Federal President, Philip McBride, sat with the South Australian delegation.

The Country Party was not present. The horse-traders remained in their stables.

Menzies had worked very hard to reach what may be called the end of stage one of his plan. He knew now that he could expect public backing if he could present himself as the leader of a convincing national party. The task in hand was to convince the eighty people in front of him that they should surrender their individualism and their separate organizations to a larger cause. He concentrated all his powers of persuasion and negotiation to this end. Standing to make his opening speech to the conference Menzies was in his full physical vigour, still dark and handsome, with an elegant touch of silver at the temples.

Because the formation of the Liberal Party of Australia may be remembered as Menzies' most important, single political achievement, what he said that afternoon deserves a little study at this point. "This Conference has been convened," he said, "in an endeavour to produce unity of organization among those who do not support socialism as the solution of Australia's political and economic problems." He gracefully dodged what he called "the merits of local controversies" and pointed out neatly that "a spirit of political revival is not always expressed by endeavouring to put new wine into old bottles."

He got down to the job in hand when he said: "The picture thus presented is one of many thousands of people all desperately anxious to travel in the same political direction but divided into various sects and bodies with no Federal structure, with no central executive, with no co-ordinated means of publicity or propaganda, and, above all, with no clearly accepted political doctrine or faith to serve as a banner under which all may fight."

Parliamentary battles, he said, could not lead on to electoral success without a common organization outside Parliament.

46

The name U.A.P. had ceased to possess any intrinsic significance. They had no adequate rank and file finance, "which
ought to be the monetary basis of any true democratic
organization".

He cut away the knots and tangles of past political errors
when he said that one organization, Australia-wide in character,
should be set up and that existing organizations should, as far
as practicable, disappear. "In a word, a new movement must
come into existence unhandicapped by vested political or
personal interests of any kind."

Turning to the question of "political faith" Menzies declared
with emphasis and clarity that the Liberal Party of today
should not forget that "there is no room in Australia for a
party of reaction." He saw more clearly than many of his predecessors that "on far too many questions we have found our
role to be simply that of the man who says, 'No'." He ended
his opening speech with a recital of party objectives as he
saw them.

Later, when the long operation of making a party organization was completed and the objectives of the Liberal Party of
Australia were formally written down, ratified and printed,
the language was the language of Menzies. He had obviously
worked intensively on his statement of objectives. His words
are enshrined in the Federal Constitution of the Liberal Party
of Australia and will remain there so long as the party endures.

Some time later one of the delegates wrote that the Canberra Conference was a "momentous success and tribute must
be paid to Mr Menzies for his discernment in convening it at
such an appropriate moment and for the genius with which he
handled it." Genius is a bold description. But something must
have set those delegates on fire. They approved the principle
of unity of policy and organization and promptly appointed
a Committee on Name and Objectives and a Committee on
Organization.

On 16th October the committees presented reports and
the delegates unanimously agreed that the name of the unified
organization should be the Liberal Party of Australia, and
adopted a broad expression of objectives. Conference also
decided that there should be a Federal organization with a

47

branch in each State, a Federal Council and a Federal Executive. A provisional executive committee was appointed to carry out conference decisions and to convene a plenary conference at which the new party would be formally constituted.

Menzies told the Press that the Canberra Conference had been remarkably successful. "The emphasis throughout was what one speaker called the need for a positive creed for a positive organization."

He has always been a good sleeper. He must have slept magnificently that night.

There were sceptics, of course, and W. M. Hughes was among them. As the late leader of the U.A.P. he croaked acidly, "To speak about unity is one thing, but to achieve it is quite another."

The Albury Conference in December 1944 formally constituted the Liberal Party of Australia and adopted a Federal Constitution. Up rose the delegates and cheered Menzies who had dominated and guided the Albury talks as smoothly as he had steered the Canberra Conference. Any disagreements were minor. What Menzies had set out to do had been accomplished. It was a brilliantly sustained effort.

He spoke at the beginning and at the end of the Albury Conference. His opening speech was a rallying political piece, with plenty of fire-crackers, Roman candles, and fine flourishes. He gazed darkly at the communists, " 'It can't happen here', says some besotted dreamer. But it can . . .", Menzies thundered. "Australia looks to us for a lead—a lead back from the abyss. . . . The ancient virtues of our character and institutions are menaced." It was heady stuff and started fires in cold bellies around Albury.

The closing speech sent them all home just as hot in the stomach. "We are going through a period of political adversity. It will be the best thing that ever happened to us. We shall fight back, we shall think back, get long views, summon our courage and stir our imagination. In that case we shall win— and if we win I believe we shall save Australia."

The date was 16th December 1944. Five long years were to pass before the opportunity came to save Australia. For five years the Australian electors, who are a rather unexcitable lot, were apparently content not to be led back from the abyss. Indeed, it is one of the ironies of politics that they took fright not so much from the fine-flowing words of Menzies but from a short terse sentence spoken by Prime Minister Chifley. But we must wait a little for that story.

IV

Philosophy at Midnight

JOHN CURTIN died on 5th July 1945. A casualty of war, he did not live to see its end. Temperamental, sensitive, and with a sense of history, he worked himself to the point of exhaustion and died in the Prime Minister's Lodge. Army Minister Forde, No. 2 on the Cabinet list of seniority, was Prime Minister for seven days. He faded from the scene when Caucus spoke its mind and on 13th July the first Chifley Ministry was sworn in.

These events were still in people's minds on 31st August 1945 when the first Federal Council of the Liberal Party of Australia met in the Assembly Hall, Sydney. It is not surprising that this important occasion in the life of the infant party made small public impact. Great events had followed one another in exhausting sequence. An Australian Prime Minister had just died. A new government had been sworn in. So the eyes of the nation were not on the Assembly Hall as the Federal President of the Liberal Party, T. Malcolm Ritchie, introduced the parliamentary leader in terms hardly calculated to provoke wild enthusiasm from his audience.

"When a man has been as long in public life as Mr Menzies," the Federal President said, "I find there is a great temptation amongst people to judge him for what he is not rather than pay proper appreciation to what he is."

That cryptic utterance was followed by one equally strange but rather more pointed: "When we are assessing a leader, it is only fair that we should give proper weight to his good points, and we should be prepared to support him with a full measure of our loyalty, for without that loyalty no leader can succeed."

Although there was some rousing stuff in the Federal President's introductory speech, the particular references to

Menzies were a reminder that in clubs and board rooms gentlemen were still looking tentatively at their new leader.

Menzies' own speech was not one of his best. Policy on a wide range of subjects still had to be worked out. After the Albury Conference the task of building a party of men and women had taken up much of his time. He had been up and down the country organizing. Meetings to form branches had been crowded and enthusiastic. By May 1945 he could announce a membership of 40,000. This figure was growing every week. Even cynical Labor politicians agreed that something was happening that could not be laughed away.

What's more, it was a curious time in our affairs. Six years of war had just ended. People were standing still for a moment, to take breath. Nevertheless, the meeting in the Assembly Hall was the official inauguration of the Liberal Party and the President was correct in saying that "we who are privileged to take part in it are starting something which has a potential beyond calculation." So now is perhaps the time to sketch for this portrait gallery the outlines of the man who had recently become Prime Minister and who would be Menzies' main political antagonist until his death.

Joseph Benedict Chifley was in his sixtieth year when he became Prime Minister. Tall and lanky, he had an Australian saunter and a good-looking Australian face under his grizzled hair. He had a steady and intelligent eye, a most engaging smile, and an air of unstudied nonchalance. His voice, full of sand and gravel, was already familiar to the public; it had been heard in the House of Representatives since 1928 when he was elected for Macquarie.

Chifley and Curtin had been close friends, although they were dissimilar in every way. Where Curtin was a creature of emotions, sometimes sunk in a black melancholia, Chifley was unflurried, unhurried, uncomplicated. Curtin's mind ranged far and wide; Chifley's interests were economic and financial. They were almost exclusively economic and financial.

Ben Chifley was an engine-driver before he became a politician. He looked like an engine-driver. In the days of steam trains many faces like Chifley's looked calmly up and down the line. He was, like his mates, a unionist, and the story goes that in the 1917 railway strike he stopped his engine at zero hour, and left it sitting on the track. No doubt he strolled back to the nearest station with a pipe in his mouth, because one could not picture Chifley without a pipe either in his mouth or in his hand.

Chifley was a frugal man. He had an enormous respect for money. He was a solid Labor man, he looked to the socialist Light on the Hill, but he had a respect for money as deep as any capitalist's. Maybe that is why he admired self-made men who built fortunes as well as industrial empires. He admired and got along well with W. J. Smith, of glass fame. Bill Smith had grown from being a bottle-blower's apprentice to the millionaire class. Like Chifley, he was a man without formal education and with a reverence for money.

Chifley's attitude to money was highly thought of in the Treasury in the years he presided over that conservative department. But his fellow ministers were not always so admiring. There was an occasion when Chifley said no to Evatt who wanted money for some External Affairs project. "It's almost impossible to get money out of Ben," Evatt complained. "You'd think it was his own."

He was frugal in his habits. While he was Treasurer to Curtin, the story got around that Chifley lunched in his office in Parliament House off a cup of tea he made on a spirit stove, and a pie. Curtin considered that such spartan fare would not sustain a Treasurer in time of war and ordered him to eat at the Hotel Kurrajong. Between sessions, he lived simply and carefully at his home town of Bathurst. His wife, amiable and reticent, was rarely seen in Canberra. Not for them the social round of the Federal capital, the diplomatic cocktail parties, afternoon tea on the lawn. He changed not at all when he became Prime Minister. He only changed rooms. And in the one, as in the other, you might find him sitting back in the chair, his feet on the table, matchbox in one hand, pipe in the other.

Curtin's death did not give rise to hectic speculation about the Labor succession. All the shrewd ones in Canberra said Chifley was a certainty. True, Army Minister Forde yearned to stay in the chair that warmed him for only a week, but this understandable ambition was not taken seriously. More serious was Evatt, then Minister for External Affairs. Evatt had not stepped down from the High Court bench to play second fiddle in politics. Ambition burned in him. It had been seen early in his Federal political career. They said that he would not have scorned a wartime National Government had he been offered the top job. Anyhow, he was hot for the top job after Curtin's death.

Chifley's friends had no doubts at all about the result. One of them, the late Bill Taylor, then a potent figure in the A.L.P. machine in New South Wales, told Chifley that he must answer the call.

Laconically, Chifley asked, "Have you got the numbers?"

"Oh, I think the numbers will be all right," replied Bill.

"Come back and tell me when you've got the numbers," said Chifley throwing another match over his shoulder.

Taylor reported back in a few days. The numbers were okay. And so Chifley became leader and Prime Minister.

Being a numbers man, of course, Chifley was in the classic Labor tradition.

All this did not alter Chifley's habits. Home at Bathurst for the weekend he would sit on his haunches and chat with his cronies. The large world did not change his ways. On a brief visit to London as Prime Minister he did not seek out the great when the job in hand was done. He sat on the Embankment and looked at the Thames. Once or twice he asserted publicly that he was a low-brow. His aesthetic sensibility was expressed in his desire to have a Brass Band in Canberra. That would have delighted him more than a Symphony Orchestra. He read a lot. From time to time he spent a whole weekend in bed reading. And he knew what he liked. He also knew what was shoddy. As Prime Minister and as leader of the Opposition he attended meetings of the Commonwealth Literary Fund, and, among the poets and learned gentry, was quite capable of saying, and saying accurately, "Well, if you don't mind, I think it's all bloody nonsense."

As Prime Minister he concentrated on economic and financial affairs, and Menzies would be the first to say that he achieved a complete mastery of them. At the time of the 1946 Federal election Chifley was also a popular leader, with a reassuring and fatherly kind of image.

Born late in 1944 and blessed and baptized in 1945, the Liberal Party was blooded at the 1946 election. Its debut on the hustings was premature, but elections have to be fought. Crusading spirit was ample enough to be bottled. High hearts and youth were there, too. So was Menzies. He led the new Liberal Party into battle against Chifley and the Labor Party. He was a politician still trying to make a comeback, not a knight in shining armour. Chifley was—or appeared to many of the voters—"safe and sound". He was depicted with some skill as "Honest Ben" and described as "the Will Rogers of Australian politics". He gazed benevolently from placards and posters, clutched his pipe, and went about like a reliable uncle.

Let us move on now to Federal election night in September 1946. The setting is the Liberal Party's State headquarters in Ash Street, Sydney. It is near midnight. The large, ground-floor office is empty. The tables are littered and the floor is strewn with scraps of paper mutely recording some phase of the night's agonizing count of votes. A few empty beer bottles and glasses tell a sad story. The air is still heavy with stale cigarette smoke. But those who had come to celebrate a victory had not remained to brood over a defeat.

Earlier in the evening the count had revealed that Menzies, leading his new Army of Liberation, would not march on Canberra. Chifley would still put his feet on the table in the Prime Minister's office, nonchalantly throwing matches over his shoulder. He had lost a few tail-feathers but his Government was safe.

The empty room in Ash Street spoke eloquently. At the far end an open door beckoned and a strange spectacle presented itself. As though posing for Rodin's *Thinker* a heavy figure was hunched in an office chair, head and arm in the classic pose. The eyes suggested profound meditation. Several seconds passed before they focused. Slowly the head was raised and William Spooner, President of the New South Wales division of the Liberal Party, sadly said: "I think there must be something wrong with our philosophy." That plaintive cry lingers in the memory because in a way it was unintentionally funny. In those days the Liberal Party had little philosophy to be wrong about. It had principles and objectives and a young organization. But philosophy and philosophers are rarely encountered in political parties. You can find strong men and weak men, programmes, policies, principles and objectives; you can find tacticians and strategists, but not philosophers.

Spooner was sad and deflated. High hopes had been dashed. It almost seemed to pessimists in a night of defeat that the young party that promised so much would fade like its forerunners. In speeches in the golden autumn of his political life Menzies frequently recalled the mood immediately following the 1946 election. "All round the club rooms in Sydney, Melbourne, even Adelaide, they began to say, 'Oh you can never win with Menzies'." And in another speech: "We weren't successful in 1946. We won a seat or two, and immediately (do you remember?) the cry arose, a muted cry, the sort of cry you hear in the corner of a club room. 'You will never win with Menzies.' This became quite a slogan, very encouraging to me as leader of the Opposition."

As before, the knockers (well-heeled, plump-bellied knockers) were wrong. They were wrong but they probably didn't care for him anyhow. One of the odd things about the political convictions of many Australians who correspond in status and riches to the English die-hard Tories is their fragility. "In a reverse kind of way," said Menzies in reminiscent mood in 1965, "it did encourage me, because it annoyed me so much that I didn't let up for years thereafter."

Return now to the melancholy Spooner. From the viewpoint of new liberalism, philosophy was not the villain. The timing was astray. Apart from the crusading of new and old Liberals the electorate was not yet decisively ready with its votes. The wartime Labor Government had not lost all its lustre in spite of strikes, shortages, black markets and all the inconveniences of an economy moving from a war to a peace footing.

But the whimsical arbiters of political fortunes, whether they sit in Heaven or in Hell, were merrily at work. Like other divine machinery, theirs worked slowly. These Fates had cast their spell upon Prime Minister Chifley and were to make him a pathfinder for Menzies. They cast Arthur Calwell in a minor role, and he played his part nobly. Up in Federal Parliament, crying out that Menzies would be an eternal leader of the Opposition, poor Arthur did not realize what the Fates were up to.

PORTRAIT GALLERY

Robert Gordon Menzies in the years of storm and stress
Ripper-Jeppersen

TOP LEFT Prime Minister
Joseph Aloysius Lyons
News & Information Bureau

LOWER LEFT The Labor Party's
James Henry Scullin who was
brought down by a Depression
News & Information Bureau

LOWER RIGHT Scullin's Treasurer,
E. G. Theodore, also caught the
great Depression
News & Information Bureau

TOP LEFT Stanley Melbourne Bruce in his urbane political years
News & Information Bureau

LOWER LEFT Earle Page, an architect and leader of the Country Party, as seen in his later, mellow years
News & Information Bureau

LOWER RIGHT William Morris Hughes, photographed in the faraway days of his Prime Ministership
News & Information Bureau

TOP LEFT Richard Gardiner Casey as the camera saw him in 1947
News & Information Bureau

LOWER LEFT Thomas Walter White, Australian Flying Corps and politics
News & Information Bureau

LOWER RIGHT The Country Party's John McEwen in the days before he reached the top
News & Information Bureau

TOP LEFT The tempestuous Archie Cameron
News & Information Bureau

LOWER LEFT Arthur Fadden in the heyday of the Menzies–Fadden coalition
News & Information Bureau

LOWER RIGHT Philip McBride, loyal friend throughout Menzies' years in Canberra
Colin Ballantyne

Eric Harrison, all the way with
R.G.M., as the 'forties saw him
News & Information Bureau

Senator George McLeay went to
Canberra in the same year as
Menzies and was constant in his
loyalty
News & Information Bureau

Wartime Prime Minister
John Curtin
News & Information Bureau

Ben Chifley as he looked when
Prime Minister
News & Information Bureau

Prime Minister Curtin with General Douglas MacArthur,
Commander-in-Chief of Allied Forces in the South-west
Pacific area in World War II   *News & Information Bureau*

Ben Chifley, with pipe, meeting one of 200 British building
workers who arrived in Canberra in January, 1947; between
them is a rather wistful-looking Arthur Calwell
News & Information Bureau

The best-known of all the
campaign photographs presents
the Menzies of 1949
Dickinson–Monteath

Herbert Vere Evatt, without
wig and gown
News & Information Bureau

TOP LEFT Senator "Bill" Spooner,
puzzled in 1946
News & Information Bureau

LOWER LEFT George Rankin, the
tough cavalier
News & Information Bureau

LOWER RIGHT E. J. ("Eddie")
Ward, the spirit of East Sydney
News & Information Bureau

Up in the Highlands of romance—near Pitlochry, Perthshire, Scotland, to be exact—in June, 1953, with Dame Pattie, daughter Heather, and the old felt hat

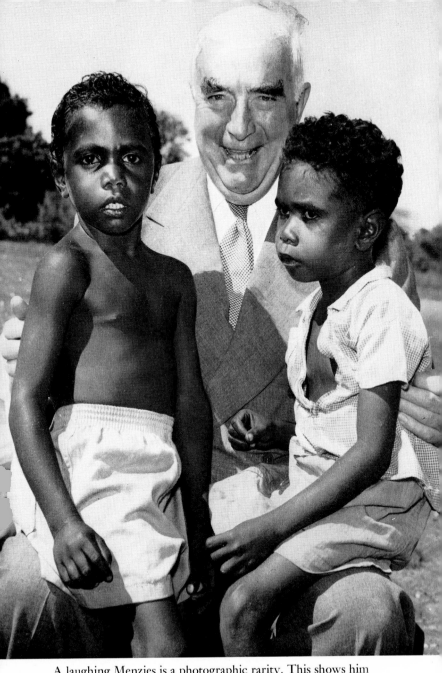

A laughing Menzies is a photographic rarity. This shows him on safari somewhere in Northern Australia   *Courier–Mail*

Arthur Calwell, for whom the
prize was so near
News & Information Bureau

Prime Minister Sir Robert Menzi
and the late President Kennedy
at the White House, Washington
in July, 1963   *U.P.I.*

The image on the TV screen dominated by the famous eyebrows

Harold Holt as Prime Minister

Athol Shmith, John Cato

Hail and farewell: the old master and the new at the
parliamentary goodbye to Sir Robert Menzies

V

Risen From the Dead

AN announcement of one sentence on 16th August 1947 was the death warrant for the Chifley Government. The author was the Prime Minister himself. "Cabinet today," the terse announcement said, "authorized the Attorney-General, Dr Evatt, and myself, to prepare legislation for submission to the Federal Parliamentary Labor Party for the nationalization of banking, other than State banks, with proper protection for shareholders, depositors, borrowers, and the state of private banks."

In a largely middle-class society this abrupt communication shocked the citizens out of their indifference to day-to-day political affairs. They had often read or been told about the Labor Party's "Socialist Objective" and had declined to take fright. Mr Curtin had been a nice man, a good man. And now Mr Chifley. He was a nice man with an honest face. That's what many dear old ladies said until they read the terrible headlines in the newspapers: BANK NATIONALIZATION.

You may take away a man's good name but not his bank.

Why did Chifley set out upon this extraordinary political course? Although nationalization of banking was in the Labor Party Platform, his Government had no mandate. The Banking Act of 1945 had given the Labor Government wide control over banking policy, but the individual still had freedom of choice. He may not have been unduly concerned about Section 48 of the Banking Act which provided that except with the consent in writing of the Treasurer, a bank could not conduct any banking business for a State or for any authority of a State, including a local governing authority. Section 48, however, began the chain reaction that blew up the Labor Government. Chifley ordered local government

57

E

bodies to conduct their business solely with the Common-wealth Bank. His regulations were challenged in the High Court by the Melbourne City Council and on 13th August 1947 the High Court decided that Section 48 was invalid.

Three days later the Prime Minister announced his intention to nationalize the banks.

Some who read the minds of prime ministers have said that Chifley had become indifferent to public opinion. It has also been said that his health was beginning to fail, that a heart condition was having its effect on his temper and his moods. Who knows? The decisive fact was the announcement. Some of Chifley's colleagues appeared to be happy enough. Arthur Calwell, a minister in the Chifley Government, told an audience in the Sydney Domain: "We are in the process of plucking the fowl, and not one feather will be put back." He was wrong. The angry leading articles in the newspapers and the dark warnings of Menzies and his colleagues about a political money monopoly were part of a swelling campaign; more ominous for Chifley was the Victorian State election which conveniently happened in November 1947. What a happening! The Cain Labor Government was heavily defeated. Inevitably, bank nationalization was the issue on which Victoria decided to pass judgment.

A month later injunctions were granted to eleven trading banks and the State Governments of Victoria, South Australia and Western Australia putting the Banking Act, 1947, on ice until the Full High Court ruled on its validity. The judgment, delivered in August 1948, declared invalid the main provisions of the Act.

Chifley was fond of saying that you can't unscramble eggs. The trading banks had been delivered, but not the Chifley Government. Doubt and suspicion replaced confidence in Honest Ben; and Menzies and the Liberal Party marched into 1949 determined to make the whole year a campaign year.

Less inflammatory than bank nationalization yet of consider-able political significance was the decision by the Federal Labor Caucus in February 1948 to increase the size of the House of Representatives from 75 to 123. This meant an increase in the Senate from 36 to 60. The case for an increase in the size of Federal Parliament was sound; not so sound was the method employed. Calwell was thought to be one of the architects of the plan, which may be summarized thus: Proportional representation for Senate voting, applied to Senators to be chosen at the next election, would guarantee Labor control of the Senate until 1953—very handy if Labor were defeated in the House of Representatives. Menzies and Fadden jointly denounced the plan. "The introduction of proportional representation for portion only of the Senate is a further illustration of the contempt which this power-drunk Government has for the rights of the electors. There is a strong case for proportional representation for the Senate, but it should apply to the whole of the Senate."

The political hazard, of course, was the House of Representatives. Increasing the House from 75 to 123, the Labor Party thought it shrewd to make safe Labor seats safer in the complete realignment of electoral divisions. It was a kindly thought to look after one's friends, a tenderness that also created a large number of marginal seats. In normal circumstances the outcome would have been unpredictable; in the climate created by the threat to nationalize the banks a Federal election for a House of 123 seats was predictably dangerous.

The auguries were unfavourable for the Labor Party in 1949. The transition from a war to a peace-time economy had not been completed. Black markets lingered on and shortages persisted. In the trade union citadels of its power, the struggle between Communists and Industrial Groupers was becoming savage. The peculiar conditions of war had given the Communist Party a special opportunity to move in on key unions. Right-wing trade unionists, particularly politically-minded Catholic unionists, had formed their own groups to contest ballots for union offices. Expecting help from the Labor Government in Canberra, they were disappointed. The more cautious of the A.L.P. politicians in the Federal capital did not want to become involved in the battle for power in the unions.

Meanwhile, strikes were a daily occurrence. The Liberal Party and the Country Party denounced these as part of "a Red plot" to paralyse industry. Conscious of its vastly increased power and influence in the trade union movement, the Communist Party branded the opposition of militant right-wingers as Catholic Action.

Television had not then come to bless us all. If the Menzies face was not as pervasive as television made it in the 'sixties, radio poured his voice and accents into ears now receptive to a Liberal Party presenting "The Case against Socialist Labor". As the 1949 election campaign came closer Prime Minister Chifley appeared to recede. The massive figure of Menzies took up more and more room. He had worked as intensively on his 1949 policy speech as he had on the principles and objectives of the Liberal Party, and it had been agreed between the Liberal and Country parties that the speech delivered on 10th November 1949 should be a policy statement on behalf of both. With the Bank Nationalization Act as a sinister backdrop and with the Communist Party as the whipping-boy, Menzies told a receptive middle-class audience that it was their year of decision.

The clear, cool voice was confident; it carried the accent of victory. "Let nobody who votes for the socialists this year be heard to complain in future that he 'didn't know it was loaded'. Above all, let those Australians who protested against the Government's banking legislation realize this. The courts have declared invalid the legislation in its present form. They have not said that the banks cannot be legally destroyed in some other way. The Government has not accepted defeat. . . . We must choose our road. Upon our decision will depend the future fate of this nation." He promised that communism would be outlawed. "The Communist Party will be declared subversive and unlawful and dissolved," he said. The joint policy speech, together with the supplementary statements, covered a spacious field, but all-important was the mood. "On December 10, we will be deciding the future of our country. It is in your hands, Australia!" Today it sounds a bit rhetorical; in 1949 it was a call to action.

In November-December of 1949 the voters looked to Menzies as ardently as they had looked to Curtin in 1943.

Chifley was an almost spectral figure in a campaign that pointed vividly to a victory for the new Liberal Party. It had attracted to its ranks and into its team of candidates young men who went into the campaign like crusaders.

Elections as decisive as that of 1949 occur infrequently. The defeat of the Bruce-Page Government in 1929 was such an election. So was the Curtin victory in 1943. The time was right for Menzies. The issue was clear-cut. It was a black and white election. There were no greys. Menzies saw his opportunity, an opportunity for which he had laboured to create the Liberal Party.

Before all the votes were counted on the night of 10th December 1949, Robert Gordon Menzies, politically, had risen from the dead. The spectacle in 30 Ash Street, Sydney, was gayer than on the Saturday night in 1946. No melancholy Jacques broodingly declared that something was wrong with the Liberal Party's philosophy. A new crop of politicians had come up in a few hours, giddy, glad, garrulous. Glasses were raised, toasts drunk. Who would want to talk about philosophy on such a night?

Increased membership of the Federal Parliament and the massive swing to the Liberal Party brought so many new faces to Canberra that the appearance of the House of Representatives was completely transformed. The old Canberra hands were a remnant of days gone by. Literally dozens of new parliamentarians crowded the lobbies when the new Parliament met. Their youthfulness was seen in eager, excited faces. Most of them had fought for their country a few years earlier, on land, on the sea and in the air. They were nearly all gallant as well as honourable members. In the early months of rapture they were consumed by a sense of purpose. The frustrations of parliamentary life were not yet apparent. In that early dawn of a new political era Robert Gordon Menzies walked among them like one of the mighty. The forty-niners were ready to remake Australia.

About him in the Ministry Menzies gathered his faithful supporters, men who had stood by him in the bad days: Eric Harrison, Harold Holt, Philip McBride, George McLeay. Country Party leader Fadden, as Treasurer, was no Earle Page, although Page himself, an extinct volcano, was given the Health portfolio.

61

In the nineteenth Parliament, which met on 22nd February 1950, Menzies, moving into his golden age, had no occasion to look behind his back. Years before, speaking at a war loan rally soon after Curtin became Prime Minister, Menzies said, "I have received many wounds from John Curtin but none of them have been in the back." In the heady 1950 days the new men he had led to Canberra were his guardsmen. The enemy sat in front of him led by Chifley, an amiable antagonist.

The folklore of the Liberal Party recalls 1949 as an *annus mirabilis*. Spectacular, indeed, was the victory of 10th December, although the Labor Party had saved a little from the disaster. In the Senate it had retained control. The Liberal Party and the Country Party had won five States in the Senate. This was not sufficient to give the Government a majority, because of the number of Labor Senators not required to face the voters in 1949. The tactics of the Labor Party were simple and understandable.

The Opposition was resolved to frustrate in the Senate the Government's legislative programme. If Government measures could not be rejected out of hand, they would be emasculated or delayed. For some time the operation was successful. Attacks and retreats in the Senate were part of the Labor Party's plan to wait for an issue which it considered politically favourable, and then to force an election on the Government. In a fascinating tactical battle Menzies out-manoeuvred the Labor Party, called the tune himself, and brought on the double dissolution election of April 1951. If 10th December 1949 was a great victory for Menzies, the election of 1951 was even more decisive as the end of a campaign.

The period between 10th December 1949 and 28th April 1951 was a seed-time that produced many of the political growths of the 'fifties. Some of them were malignant. They were menacing to the leaders of the Labor Party rather than to Menzies whose personality had been shaped with nearly all the final touches by the years in Opposition. The beginning of 1951 was an uneasy time. Inflationary pressures were increasing ominously and prices were rising. Chifley, with his respect for what he called the hip-pocket nerve, tried to turn the 1951 campaign into an argument about inflation and prices.

The concept was orthodox. Bread and butter elections were often successful.

Unfortunately for Chifley the issue of communism had been enlarged to portentous dimensions. Menzies had promised in 1949 to outlaw the Communist Party and had introduced his Communist Party Dissolution Bill into Parliament. The Government then introduced two bills to amend the Conciliation and Arbitration Act. One was to enable the Court to command obedience to its awards by injunction. The other was for the election of trade union officers by secret ballot. In his 1951 policy speech Menzies said that this secret ballot legislation was designed to ease "the task of those non-communist unionists who desire to challenge a ballot on the ground of actual or anticipated irregularities".

During the campaign the Labor M.P. for Gellibrand (Mr Mullens) said at Footscray: "I am in favour of the Menzies legislation for secret ballots and I will do all I can to convert other members of the Labor Party to this viewpoint."

A few days later the Melbourne *Age* began the report of an election meeting this way:

> Blows were struck and an interjector was pushed from the hall during a lively election meeting at Williamstown last night.
>
> The interjector had cried, "You dog!" to Mr Mullens, Labor candidate and sitting member for Gellibrand, when Mr Mullens was making a vitriolic attack on communism.
>
> Mr Mullens said: "The communists in Australia are spies, saboteurs and disrupters of our industry and our economy."
>
> Mr Mullens said the Communist Party should be wiped out, abolished, its funds taken, and it should disappear from the country.

During question time an irate A.L.P. supporter shouted: "I brand Mr Mullens as a supporter of Menzies."

"If I had ten thousand votes I would use them all to vote for the dissolution of the Communist Party," retorted Mullens.

The episode was one of the earliest public manifestations of the civil war soon to break out in the Labor Party. It passed with little notice in the rough and tumble of an election campaign. An alert electorate, however, sensed that the Labor Party was divided on the question of communism and without a coherent policy. Menzies had pointed the bone in Parliament shortly before the opening of the campaign. He was speaking on the High Court's decision on the Communist Party Dissolution Act. "There can be no strong and effective government, either legislative or administrative, in the Commonwealth until the conflict over these matters has been resolved, and a government is in office which with a majority in both Houses can promptly put its proposals with effect by legislation and by clear and strong executive action."

It remains to be said that next day Menzies forced the challenge in the Senate. The Government had asked for a decision on the Commonwealth Bank Bill, which, in the circumstances of the day, was relatively unimportant. When the Labor Opposition, using their Senate majority, referred the Bill to a Select Committee, the Government said this was "failure to pass" as required by Section 57 of the Constitution. On 15th March Menzies asked the Governor-General for a double dissolution and got it.

On 28th April 1951 the electors gave the Menzies Government control of both Houses. The Prime Minister had displayed his skill as a political tactician. He had disclosed his very remarkable sense of timing. He showed friends and enemies that he was prepared to take calculated risks when the prize was big enough. He had confounded his critics to become Prime Minister a second time; he had out-manoeuvred the Labor Party tacticians to win control of both Houses.

On 13th June 1951 Joseph Benedict Chifley died. Like Curtin he died on the job. He had recognized the danger signs in his party. He knew that men of lifelong loyalty to the A.L.P. were taking sides on the Left and the Right. In his own blunt way he probably believed that the trouble could be resolved within the party. The task of holding the Labor Party together passed to a new Federal parliamentary leader. Dr Evatt now takes his place in this gallery of portraits as Menzies' antagonist in the years of the Prime Minister's abundant power. Never has the Australian political scene presented us with such a contrast.

The story of the 1951 campaign ends with a summing up. On 8th May the *Sydney Morning Herald* headed its main leading article, "Unhappy Plight of the Labour Party", and this is what the article said:

Progress counting in the Federal election has stamped the defeat of Labour as even more decisive than the early returns indicated. The party's fortunes are, in fact, at their lowest ebb since the depression days. It emerges with its policies rejected, its control of the Senate lost, its ranks divided, its leadership discredited.

On the credit side, the Opposition has nothing to show but gains in a handful of marginal seats. These wins still leave it hopelessly inferior in the House of Representatives. And they were mainly due, not to any broad approval of Labour's programme, but to sectional resentment of the Government's wool levy and wheat policy. On the big national issues, Labour was repudiated. Mr Menzies would have been well content to trade more seats than he has lost for his now certain majority in the Senate.

Mr Chifley, on the contrary, has cause for discontent, even dismay, in almost every aspect of the poll. In New South Wales, the ('key')—and his own—State, Labour was soundly beaten. The Liberals actually increased their vote in the urban electorates where the Opposition had hoped to gain ground, especially on the prices issue. Dr Evatt's moral defeat in Barton came as a particularly heavy blow. By contrast, the better showing in Victorian industrial constituencies brought no comfort to Mr Chifley since the chief beneficiaries were those Labour members who had resisted the Chifley-Evatt line on communism.

Overall, the defeat Labour has suffered is, in the circumstances of 1951, sharper than its rejection in 1949; and the re-affirmation of Mr Menzies' mandate is correspondingly strong. The Opposition, in the first place, has paid the penalty of its arrogant obstruction in the Senate. The majority it had engineered there could have been used over the full term of Parliament as a check and brake on Government legislation. This advantage, so potentially valuable to the Labour Party, has been rashly thrown away.

Sheer obstruction proved a fatal strategic error. Of the Opposition's tactical blunders Mr Menzies also took skilful advantage. Out-manoeuvred in Parliament, it might still have been preserved from disaster in the field, had Mr Chifley put forward a coherent and courageous policy, instead of a hotch-potch of promises and half-promises, compromises, and negatives. He was, of course, handicapped by the open divisions in his party on such vital issues as communism, secret ballots in trade unions, and national defence. Himself a convinced socialist, he played down the A.L.P. socialist policy; tried vainly to switch attention to inflation; and, on what was the crucial issue of the campaign, mumbled awkwardly about there being two sorts of communism.

The upshot is that Labour today, disunited and frustrated, has lost its hold on the voters who formerly put and kept it in power. It will not regain favour without a radical change of outlook. In the popular mind, it is tainted with communism, through its dependence on the big communist-controlled unions, to say nothing of its Deputy Leader's legal espousal of communist causes. On defence, too, clinging to obsolete ideas, it is utterly out of step with national feeling. Labour will have to jettison its unrealistic and isolationist policies before any part of its credit can be restored with electors who have turned to the Liberal and Country parties for protection against the nation's internal and external enemies.

Part Three

HONOURABLE GENTLEMEN

I

Politicians Are Human

IN SPITE of popular belief and prejudice, politicians are human. As a small tribe in the national collection politicians are not exotic. There are not more wicked politicians than wicked grocers. Proportionally, there are more rogues in King's Cross than in Canberra. Politicians are not larger or smaller, brighter or duller, than lawyers or plumbers. If more members of parliament appear to be more pompous than some of the bores one meets about town, the stage setting of politics may provide the reason. It encourages a little flatulence and a platitudinous manner. For the will to survive is strong. A politician is not hanged for what he doesn't say. Truth can be fatal politically, the platitude rarely.

The visitor to Canberra, craning from the public gallery in the House of Representatives, will be disappointed if he expects to see row after row of brilliant and gifted men. Parliament is a cross-section. Parliamentary life would be intolerable if all the members were eggheads. It would be equally intolerable if they were all lawyers or all poets. In a rough and ready way Parliament manages to be fairly representative of the people it represents.

Some of us find it difficult enough to fit into life; the politician has to fit into Parliament—and this institution, cradled in England, has about it some of the eccentricity of the English. The two-party system of parliamentary government seems curiously English. Regular parties first appeared in English history in the reign of Charles II. From the beginning each party was offensive to the other. The King's men called their opponents Whigs, a rude name for Scottish highwaymen. The Whigs, who stood in Parliament for the aristocratic oligarchy, branded their opponents as Tories, and a Tory was an Irish pirate who inhabited the Tory Islands some miles off the coast of Donegal.

True, the nineteenth century saw the full establishment both of parliamentary and party government in Britain; but party government then was very different from party government now. The House of Commons was still a gentlemen's club. Members were not paid. They behaved as they pleased. Some of them remembered Mr William Pitt interrupting a speech to be sick behind the Speaker's Chair. He had been dining and wining with his friend Mr Dundas.

Many members of Parliament in the eighteenth and in the first half of the nineteenth century never delivered even a maiden speech. They were silent not from timidity or lack of words. They considered it vulgar to make speeches in public and an impertinence for anybody to expect a gentleman to explain himself. Gentlemen members from the counties left the talking to "outsiders" like Disraeli or Gladstone. Parliament itself only sat for a small part of the year. This suited the honourable gentlemen who regarded the institution's prime role as the preserver of privilege. Party lines were not drawn as sharply as they now are. A Tory could turn Whig and go back to the Tories without a quizzing glance being raised.

Party organizational machinery was tentatively introduced after the Reform Bill of 1867 which extended the franchise. The idea of a nation-wide party organization with a central office came from Disraeli and his novel approach to political organization created the Conservative victory of 1874.

This slight excursion into political history is designed to assist the layman's understanding of the parliamentary institution and the honourable gentlemen who adorn it. Parliamentary government and the two-party system are commonly regarded as peculiarly and magnificently English. They have also handed down to our own generation of politicians in Australia some lusty traditions.

George Rankin, who was first elected to the House of Representatives in 1937 and who later transferred to the Senate, at once comes to mind. He would have been a match for the hard-riding and hard-drinking gentlemen who rolled back to the Commons after a dinner washed down copiously with claret. General Rankin was a commander of Light Horse in World War I, a veteran of Gallipoli. He was a man of great physical strength, great loyalties, and great quality. He didn't have much to say in Parliament. At table or with a drink in his hand, he was a good companion, a man of large appetites.

Occasionally, visitors from General Rankin's constituency appeared in Canberra and, naturally, called on him. Always hospitable, he showed them around and then escorted them to the bar. There was the day when other members saw the General talking of old times with three visiting constituents. Rankin was not a boastful man. He was, indeed, excessively modest. Convivial friends, however, stimulated him and his anecdotes took on a large and dramatic air. This time he was describing a cavalry charge against the Turks. The three constituents were spellbound. They could see it all, the whole panorama of battle.

"And then, suddenly, right in front of me loomed up an enormous Turk, a giant," said Rankin, gesticulating a little. He paused for dramatic effect.

One of the visitors, a small, eager man, asked tensely, "What did you do, General?"

"I cut off his bloody head," replied Rankin and took another sip of his beer.

Of the Queenslanders Arthur Fadden was the most authentic, a man with an enormous zest for living. In the Menzies era four men led the Country Party in Canberra: the wily Earle Page, the tempestuous and uncertain Archie Cameron, then Fadden, and, after him, John McEwen, strong-willed and moody. Fadden was Acting Prime Minister and Treasurer. Because of the duration of Menzies' prime ministership he was Acting P.M. while Menzies was out of the country for longer than some men had been Prime Minister. He could be relied upon to keep affairs running smoothly. With Fadden in control Menzies could go off knowing that even if the mice played their activities would be innocuous. Fadden's loyalty to the Coalition was very real. Among all the top personalities in the Country Party during the Menzies régime Fadden was the only one who tried hard and sincerely to bring about an amalgamation between the Liberal and Country parties on the Federal parliamentary level.

He was a hard-working Treasurer and knew the job. In the early 'fifties it was anything but a popular job. Inflationary pressures did not make for happy Budgets and the laments of the taxpayers were loud in the Treasurer's ears.

"I could have had a meeting of all my friends and supporters in a one-man telephone booth," Fadden would say.

He was not a man to brood over the critics after the day's work. His particular musketeers were Bernie Corser, another Queenslander, and Tom Collins, M.P. for Hume. They were a formidable trio and practical jokers with almost a touch of genius. One night at the Hotel Canberra they staged a "Country Party crisis" for the fun of watching the newspapermen's reactions. The stunt was so convincingly carried out in the corridors and lounge of the hotel—with telephone calls and solemn mysterious conferences in corners—that the journalists were filing copy about a crisis that existed only in the imagination of Fadden and his exuberant playboys.

Fadden could not resist a wisecrack. In 1941, while he was Acting Prime Minister, he called a press conference in Sydney. Basing his comments on what he regarded as correct information, he spoke of the inevitability of conflict with Japan. The conference in these circumstances was sombre. Fadden closed the conference with the usual formula, "Well, that's all boys." Then, as they stood to leave, he said, with a wry grin, "I always knew I'd finish up pulling a rickshaw!" It was typical Fadden.

His memory was elephantine and his collection of stories, Irish, Greek, Italian, Australian, anything you name, was prodigious. He told them well and he never tired of telling them. Nobody in Canberra could take off Billy Hughes more amusingly than Fadden. Indeed, Hughes will live so long as Fadden is around to tell the Hughes stories, cupping his ear, and catching the Hughes accent perfectly.

"I remember the day," Fadden would say, "when I overheard two dear old ladies who were being taken on a tour of Parliament House. They had fallen behind the others and were looking at that bronze bust of Billy in King's Hall. One of the old girls said to the other, 'Dear me, I didn't know Mr Hughes was a coloured man!' "

Or Fadden would say: "Did you hear the one about Billy's touring in Victoria when he was P.M.? He was being entertained to lunch by one of the shire councils. The shire president was pointing out to Billy the various officers round the table. One had a big red nose—a nose of unmistakable hue. 'He,' said the president, 'is the chairman of our local water board.' Little Billy gazed at the nose. 'Ah, yes,' he said, 'a most excellent choice. You could trust him with any amount of water.' "

Fadden might then tell of the night at the Russian Embassy when Hughes, a modest drinker, was snared by a very potent brew of vodka. Fadden was with Hughes. Page was there also. Above them were portraits of Stalin, Churchill, and Roosevelt. Gazing up at them and clutching his vodka, Hughes gave tongue. "Every sip of this extraordinary concoction fills me with an increasing admiration for Churchill," said Hughes. "Yes, brother, every sip. He must be a very remarkable man to drink this stuff just to please that so-and-so Stalin." Fortunately, the interpreter did not get the message very clearly to the Ambassador, and shortly afterwards Hughes and his friends retired from the scene. The night air smote Hughes. Clutching Fadden's arm, he said. "Support me, Artie. I am sinking into the ground."

Two great Hughes stories date back to his splendid years as a wartime Prime Minister. The setting is London and Hughes is being escorted to Buckingham Palace by Winston Churchill and Sir Alfred Mond. Australia's Prime Minister is to be made a Privy Councillor by King George the Fifth in person.

"After he's done it," said Churchill, "he will talk a little. But you must not lead the conversation. The King will lead."

71

Hughes said he understood the protocol.

"Well, brother," he said, "after it was over we did indeed talk. We were in a large room with windows overlooking the Palace gardens. Remember that it was wartime. His Majesty gazed out and observed the growing vegetables. 'You see,' he remarked, 'we have been growing some vegetables.' Then the poor fellow dried up. Yes, brother, he dried up. Well, what could I do? I saw a great sword hanging on the wall and I said, 'That's a very interesting looking sword, Your Majesty.' And do you know, my friend, a light came into his eyes and he spoke about that bloody sword for half an hour."

About the same time Hughes was making his first official visit to No. 10 Downing Street. For most men this would have been an historic event. In the car with Hughes was an Australian friend whom he had entertained to lunch. The dish had been chicken, which Hughes had not touched. Dyspeptic, he had touched very little.

As the car moved on towards No. 10 through the streets of history Hughes said to his friend, "While you were eating that chicken I was thinking of the early days when I carried my swag. I had a mate and we sometimes employed a most successful device to provide ourselves with a meal. We might sight a promising property and carry out a reconnaissance to establish the important fact that there were chickens at the rear of the homestead. My friend would move stealthily toward the birds while I would approach the front of the house, make myself known to the lady of the house, and entertain her with witty observations while my colleague caught the bird. This, brother, is a difficult feat requiring expert skill. You seize the chicken and wring its neck in the one movement. . . . Ah, my friend, here we are at Downing Street, I must leave you here."

Characters like Hughes were, of course, rare. Everything he did carried his signature. In his U.A.P. days, before air travel was the thing, he would often drive to and from Canberra. His wife and secretary were accustomed to these adventures. Others would speak shudderingly of their experiences. Leaving the Hotel Canberra bound for Sydney, he would put his foot on the accelerator and leave it there. His head barely appeared above the wheel. Chickens, cats, dogs, pedestrians had to move fast. He went like a rocket.

There was a time after the stormy days of the 'forties when in the name of unity a reconciliation seemed desirable between Menzies and Hughes. The delicate task of arranging the meeting fell to Fadden who could talk to Hughes when others were turned away. A reluctant Hughes finally consented and was guided to Menzies' room. Courtesies were exchanged and the pipe of peace symbolically smoked.

Departing, and with the door scarcely closed behind him, Hughes said in that voice he could throw across a theatre, "But I still think he's a big bastard!"

F

II

The Menzies-Evatt Confrontation

AFTER Chifley's death Herbert Vere Evatt was elected Federal parliamentary leader of the Labor Party and became Menzies' No. 1 political antagonist. The long conflict between them was an absorbing study. Both were bred to the law, one becoming a leader of the Bar, the other a High Court judge. Each had a large capacity for sustained work, scholarship, intelligence of high order, and great ambition. Menzies could have been described without gross exaggeration as an imperialist and a conservative, Evatt as a socialist with republican leanings. Towards each other they were more than party leaders on opposing sides. They were also opponents in a strong personal sense. Each reciprocated the dislike of the other.

Seen on the floor of the House they were utterly dissimilar in appearance and style. Comparisons were easy to make because they sat at the table opposite each other, only the width of the table apart. Menzies, as everybody knows, was tall as well as massive, elegantly white-haired in the years of his jousting with Evatt, who was heavily built but stocky, with grizzled hair. The Prime Minister, no Brummell in the matter of dress, was always neat. Evatt was invariably untidy. Nicknames can't be avoided in Canberra and to some of his political opponents Evatt was Shaggy Mick. On nights when he was on the list to make an important speech he would enter the House burdened with papers, books, and notes. By the time he ended his speech the floor near him might be strewn with discarded notes, the table covered with books, cuttings, and who knows what of jottings and scraps. By contrast, Menzies usually had a neat handful of headline reminders.

Evatt concentrated on what he had to say, not on how to

say it. His voice had no tonal variety and wearied the ear. He spent little time on phrase-making, working exclusively on material and argument. The Menzies' timing, style, and colour were wholly missing.

Although his ministerial record marked him as a logical successor to Chifley, he was an unusual choice for a Labor Party rooted in trade unionism. To Labor's rank-and-file he was an intellectual, and that was not a virtue. Scullin, Curtin and Chifley were seen in a recognizable mould; the Evatt type seemed, and was, unpredictable. The sudden descent from the High Court bench, a place remote from the tug of ambition and the back-room intrigues of politics, made Evatt headline news in 1940. And from that year until the end he was rarely out of the headlines.

As schoolboys both Evatt and Menzies made their own way. Money and influence opened no gates for them. Their brilliance as scholars was the key. Glittering honours were won by Evatt at the University of Sydney where he graduated in law with rare distinction. In 1929 he was a K.C., in 1930 a Justice of the High Court. Before this, politics had attracted him and he sat as the Labor member for Balmain in the New South Wales Parliament from 1925 until his appointment to the High Court. His State apprenticeship to politics was unspectacular. The flourishes of later years were absent.

Yet the political virus had such a hold that his eminent position in the world of law was insufficient to satisfy his restless mind, his ego and his will for power. After a decade on the Himalayan heights of the High Court he elected to quit those tranquil altitudes and become a politician again, this time with the prime ministership as his goal. How could it have been otherwise? He had reached the top of a great profession. He had made a distinguished name for himself. Who could believe that all this would be cast aside for the role of a Labor Party back-bencher in Canberra? Evatt was driven to climb to the top in politics. But neither he nor those who cheered his decision understood, in 1940, that Evatt's temperament was ill-suited to politics. Events were also to show that his flair and his political judgement were less than his ambition. Nor did he see when he made his choice that the decisive conflict would be between himself and Menzies, whose taste for the great game had been sharpened by bitter experience. All this was hidden from Evatt.

Sometimes Fortune is whimsical. It was odd that the fall of Menzies in 1941 was a prelude to Evatt's rise. He was a member of the Curtin War Cabinet. Later he was deputy to Prime Minister Chifley. He represented Australia at the birth of the United Nations Organization. Always a passionate champion of UNO, he believed that it was the answer to war. In the year that saw the fall of the Chifley Government, Evatt was President of the General Assembly of the United Nations. It was perhaps the pinnacle of his political career. After Chifley's death in 1951 Evatt was elected leader of the Opposition and, for him, this was the beginning of the last stage of his journey to the Prime Minister's office. In fact, it was the end as well as the beginning. Fortune can be cruel as well as whimsical. For the prize was to be almost within his grasp—almost.

On 4th September 1951 Menzies opened his campaign for a "Yes" vote on the Government's proposal to alter the Constitution so that it might have power to outlaw the Communist Party. At the Federal election of 1949 Menzies had foreshadowed his proposals for banning the Communist Party. His Government had introduced the Communist Party Dissolution Bill which ultimately was passed by both the House of Representatives and the Senate. Challenged in the High Court the Communist Party Dissolution Act was declared to be beyond the power of the Commonwealth Parliament. Hence the referendum of 22nd September 1951.

"You now have a chance to arm your National Parliament with power to deal with our most dangerous internal foe," said Menzies. "If you reject it, it will not come again. This is the one great chance. . . . I call upon the Australian people to cast a 'Yes' vote on September 22."

On 22nd September, however, the Australian people cast a "No" vote. After the victory of 1949 and the double triumph of April 1951, Menzies was in a mood of high confidence. The September "No" hit him hard. The rejection hurt all the more because leading the fight for "No" was Evatt, who, naturally, was jubilant. He had not only successfully campaigned for the defeat of the referendum; he had led for certain unions when the Communist Party Dissolution Act was challenged in the High Court. All along he had opposed Menzies on the communist issue. As 22nd September approached the giant antagonists were the Prime Minister and the leader of the Opposition. The whole country was in a ferment and furiously divided, but above the lesser debaters the two Olympians dominated the scene.

What manner of victory was this for Evatt? And what kind of a defeat for Menzies? From now until the end of his political life Evatt would be branded as the friend of the communists. Mockery from the Left would depict Menzies as a red-baiter and as a smooth old magician producing pink rabbits from the hat whenever election time came round. These labels were of less significance than the mood of the political parties. Menzies had behind him a party unanimous in the belief that the Communist Party should be banned. Behind Evatt, however, the A.L.P. ranks were divided. The very success of Evatt's campaign against the Communist Referendum, and his advocacy in the High Court, deepened the discontent inside the Labor Party. The later rounds in the conflict between Menzies and Evatt can be understood in detail only if the malaise in the A.L.P. is also understood.

Communism was the cause of the sickness. To trace its origins one goes back to the years of World War II. Cleverly and with tireless resolve, the Communist Party of Australia had penetrated deeply into key trade unions. Some of its ablest members were in command of unions. Campaigns inside the Trade Union movement to break the power and influence of the Communist Party were futile until the Industrial Groups came into being. Originally, "the Groupers", as they were described, were predominantly Roman Catholic trade unionists who had a religious as well as an industrial reason for organizing to promote their own candidates for trade union office. The struggle for power in the unions was long and bitter. Inevitably, it influenced the A.L.P. parliamentarians. In its early years the Australian Labor Party, although not a party of Roman Catholics, did attract many men with a working-class political outlook and a Roman Catholic faith. Always turbulent, the A.L.P. had argued, brawled, and sometimes split on economic and other material issues; not until the 'fifties was it in danger of splitting on the ground of faith. The grassroot argument between communists and industrial groupers was echoed in Federal Caucus between Left and Right when the Communist Party Dissolution Bill was debated. It was as much a religious as a political argument. Chifley knew how dangerous this kind of dispute could be. A few weeks before his death he spoke about the dissension in the party. His audience was the Annual Conference of the N.S.W. Division of the A.L.P.

Evatt inherited the leadership; he also inherited the factions. Savouring victory after the September 1951 referendum vote, he looked forward with relish to the next Federal election. Some of the ardent Roman Catholics in his party were critical, but the test of leadership was victory—and in this Evatt ardently believed.

His prestige was high at this stage. Australians, disinterested in the day-to-day intrigues of politics, had views on communism; but many of them thought of Evatt as a humanitarian, a hard fighter for the underdog, a champion of civil liberties, a man who had stepped down from the High Court because there was a man's work to be done in the places of government. Inside the party the assessment was closer because the politicians working with him knew him both as a man and as a politician. And as a man he was complex. Away from politics he could be tolerant, sympathetic, generous. Inside politics he was suspicious, authoritarian. Curtin had sensed the lust for power in Evatt. Chifley, too, had observed him closely. His private nickname for his Minister for External Affairs was "Ivan the Terrible", and he would say it with a grin.

In the close world of the Labor Party, which puts a mystical value on the word mateship, Evatt did not encourage close friendship. If he was suspicious of those who wanted to help and be friendly, the fault was in his own strange make-up. The pattern of his personality was not seen as a whole until years later, not until the breakdown.

He was an eccentric. One might encounter him on the

Melbourne-Sydney express, heavily rugged and wearing a hat or two. He was on guard against chills. Germs were conspiring to assault him. It was a queer experience to watch him warding off these phantoms. There were other oddities. He was constantly at war with aircraft. He distrusted them. On one strange journey in the war years the United States Air Force provided him with a plane from the East to the West Coast. He was bound for Washington. The aircraft came down to refuel at night in the middle of the continent. The strip was some miles from anywhere. Suddenly, Evatt's dislike for the aircraft erupted in a refusal to renew any further association with the monster. The situation, embarrassing for his staff, was worse for the American officials. It was wartime and aircraft were scarce. However, another machine was conjured up. It arrived. Half-way across to it, Evatt propped. He didn't like its look. And he said so. He refused to board the plane. Some time later Evatt and his staff were driven by car to the nearest railhead. Stubborn, angry, frustrated, the Minister for External Affairs completed his journey to Washington by train.

He had a fixation about the seat nearest the crew's quarters. This could be difficult when he was travelling on a commercial plane. One day in Canberra he stalked late into the aircraft and demanded the seat at the top of the plane. It was occupied by a placid citizen who had paid his fare and who had been allotted his seat. He did not propose to give it up or remove himself to another seat for anybody, particularly not for Dr Evatt. The air hostess tried to sort things out. Evatt stood and glared; the passenger sat and stared. Twenty minutes late the aircraft took off. Evatt was in the other fellow's seat.

In short, he was unusual; and the condition the Labor Party found itself in demanded leadership that was safe, normal, tactful, compromising. Instead, the A.L.P. politicians in Canberra had chosen to lead them back to the promised land a brilliant, eccentric, explosive, unpredictable intellectual. After Jim Scullin, that kindly old warrior, after the lonely, dedicated John Curtin, after phlegmatic, down-to-earth Ben Chifley, Herbert Vere Evatt was the oddest thing that had ever happened to them.

But, until a certain April day in 1954, Caucus believed that he could and would be Prime Minister of Australia.

In the early 'fifties the Menzies Government was not beloved by the multitude; in many board rooms it was bitterly criticized. Being rude about the Government was the expected thing at lunch and brightened the cocktail hour. The cause of it all was inflation. The opportunists were riding the whirlwind of rising prices in the hope of profit. Naturally they didn't like the Government's economic and financial policies—restrictions, heavy taxation, credit controls. The climate in early 1953 was not favourable for a Senate election, but it could not be avoided. Although the election of May 1953 was exclusive to the Senate, it was of critical importance for Menzies. He had won control of the Senate in 1951; he was in danger of losing that control in 1953. A government which had courted unpopularity with its economic policy could not expect to be rewarded with votes. Evatt and his colleagues, smelling the wind, went about hinting at mass unemployment and other horrors. The poll on 9th May was very close. Like the Battle of Waterloo, it was for Menzies a "near-run thing". Queensland remained faithful and the Prime Minister retained control of the Senate, narrowly.

A few months after the Senate election the Menzies Government brought down a pretty spectacular tax-reduction Budget. Some of the clouds had rolled by. The sour looks on the faces of the businessmen had changed to smiles. The Labor Party's prophecies of disaster did not sound so terrible. But the memory of discontent was sufficiently potent to encourage the Labor Party as it prepared for the Federal election set down for 29th May 1954. The A.L.P. tacticians decided to make it a social welfare election. Evatt was to promise abolition of the Means Test within three years, to increase pensions immediately, to increase child endowment, reduce taxation. Many other promises were worked into a policy speech full of allure and glitter.

On 13th April all the political parties were organizing for the May election and the twentieth Parliament was coming peacefully to a close. "April is the cruellest month," wrote T. S. Eliot, but Eliot is not widely read in Parliament House,

Canberra. So unruffled was the April day that Opposition leader Evatt had gone off to Sydney to be guest of honour at the annual reunion of the Old Fortians; he was a Fort Street old boy.

At eight o'clock that night Prime Minister Menzies rose and said to an astonished House: "Some days ago one Vladimir Mikhailovich Petrov who has been Third Secretary in the Soviet Embassy in Australia since February 1951 voluntarily left his diplomatic employment and made to the Australian Government, through the Australian Security Intelligence Organization, a request for political asylum. The Director-General of the Australian Security Intelligence Organization, acting under the authority of myself, the Attorney-General and the Department of External Affairs, received this request. The request has been granted, and, following the established diplomatic practice, protection has been provided to Mr Petrov. The Soviet Embassy has been notified accordingly."

The startled members then heard the Prime Minister say that enough material from Petrov had been examined to show "that there are matters affecting Australia's security which call for judicial investigation". He said that the Government proposed to set up a Royal Commission.

Next morning Evatt told the House that the Labor Party would support an inquiry. A Labor Government, he declared, would "see that no guilty person escapes and that no innocent person is condemned, and that the whole matter is dealt with free from all question of party politics." He also said that he would have cancelled his engagement in Sydney had he known of the Prime Minister's announcement.

Later in the day Menzies introduced the Royal Commission Bill, a short measure making it clear that the Commissioners would have power to compel the attendance of witnesses. In an obvious reply to Evatt, who had pointed out that an election was coming up, Menzies agreed that ". . . happening as it does through circumstances beyond our control not long before a general election, some people might be disposed to think it has some electoral significance." Loftily, he put aside such uncharitable speculation! "I want to make it abundantly clear that this concerns something far superior to party."

The subsequent proceedings before the Royal Commission on Espionage disclosed that Petrov defected on 3rd April 1954. For £5000 he handed over certain documents, most of which were in Russian. Although these details were not revealed until later, Mrs Petrov became front-page news a week after Menzies made his startling announcement to Parliament. On 19th April Mrs Petrov was driven to Mascot airport to board a plane for Darwin en route for Moscow under the guard of two armed Soviet couriers. The news of her intended departure had become known. At the airport a crowd demonstrated angrily. They shouted warnings to her. The message was, "Don't go back to Russia." She spent an unhappy and sleepless night on the plane, filled with fear and uncertainty.

It was a hectic night on many levels. Up at the Prime Minister's Lodge in Canberra decisions had to be taken—and taken quickly. So it happened that the captain of the aircraft, high above the clouds, was asked to discover, if he could, what Mrs Petrov's wishes were. Mr Leydin, the Acting Administrator of the Northern Territory, was instructed at midnight to interview Mrs Petrov when the plane touched down at Darwin Airport.

This was good, exciting, spy stuff and it all came out in the newspapers.

The captain of the plane radioed Canberra his impression that Mrs Petrov desired to stay in Australia, but was afraid, and that she had told him her guards were armed.

In the Darwin dawn pistols were flourished and Mrs Petrov's guards disarmed. The distraught woman knew not what to do or say. She feared her husband was dead.

The wires were busy again. Canberra moved fast, and, at 7 a.m., just before the plane was due to resume its flight, Petrov in Sydney spoke to his wife in Darwin. He said he was well and free and urged her to stay in Australia.

"I will stay," said Mrs Petrov, and that was that, all very dramatic, sensational, and in the style the public expected. The citizens read their newspapers avidly.

The incidental fact that a Federal election was coming up on 29th May was, perhaps, forgotten in the excitement. It happened, however, that on 4th May Prime Minister Menzies opened his campaign. He didn't mention Petrov. He spoke not a word about the Royal Commission throughout the campaign.

However, the Royal Commission on Espionage opened its sittings in Canberra on 17th May and sat there until 19th May. Counsel outlined the general nature of the matters with which the Commission was required to deal, an outline that whetted the public's appetite. But the hearing of evidence did not begin until 30th June, and by that time the general election of 1954 was over and Menzies was still Prime Minister. It had been a hard-fought campaign. Early on polling night the A.L.P. was doing well and, as the count progressed, the outcome looked a little obscure. Menzies was following the count from his suite at the Windsor Hotel, in Melbourne. It was eleven o'clock before he could put aside his notes and light a cigar. The Labor Party had won seats from him but had not won the election.

Afterwards, when all the votes had been counted, and the post-mortem completed, one name grew large and sinister in Evatt's mind and in the minds of his supporters. One name: Petrov. It became a terrible name for Evatt. He had seen the prime ministership in his hands. He had worked night and day through an exhausting campaign. What had defeated him? In these dark moods rational explanations are not welcomed. There are no second prizes in an election. You win or you lose. Evatt lost. His opponent, the Prime Minister, had not spoken Petrov's name in the campaign. But others had, and the newspapers were full of it.

The name Petrov leads us on to another strange episode in Evatt's political career.

In August 1954 Evatt was given leave to appear before the Royal Commission. There is little point now in reciting the immediate reasons for his intervention. One may fairly believe that he sincerely conceived the theory that he and the Australian Labor Party were the victims of a political conspiracy. Day after day, with that in mind, he cross-examined the witnesses before the Royal Commission. On 7th September 1954 his permission to appear was withdrawn and on 21st October 1954 the Commissioners made an Interim Report to the Government. This report stated that charge had followed charge with bewildering variations, that suggestions had been made of blackmail, forgery, uttering, fabrication, fraud and conspiracy. "Although, in the result, all the charges turned out to be fantastic and wholly unsupported by any credible evidence," the Commissioners said, "they were grave and necessitated patient judicial inquiry by us."

The Interim Report of the Commissioners was dated 21st October 1954. On 5th October 1954—these dates are suggestive and illuminating—Evatt, as Federal parliamentary leader of the Labor Party, brought his Party's discontents into the open by publishing a statement attacking "a small minority of Labor members, located particularly in the State of Victoria", whom he accused of "disloyal and subversive action". He stated that he would refer the matter to the next meeting of the Federal Executive of the A.L.P. with a view to action being taken at the Federal A.L.P. Conference in January 1955.

Imagine Evatt's state of mind. Throughout his appearance before the Royal Commission he had been emotional and over-wrought. He believed passionately that he had been the victim of a conspiracy. He believed that trickery, black magic or something damnable had cheated him of the prime minister-ship. Detesting his political opponents on the government side and Menzies in particular, he mortally hated those in his own party who had rallied to the Industrial Groupers in their fight against the communists in the trade unions. The Right and the Left of the A.L.P. had been snarling at each other for years. His enemies in the Labor Party were gloating over his humilia-tion before the Royal Commission. Furious, tired, implacable, he declared open war and in that statement of 5th October 1954 he split the Labor Party. He began a deadly conflict that has never ended. Sneeringly, the Victorian secretary of the A.L.P. said that the attack "appears to be motivated by Dr Evatt's difficulties before the Royal Commission on Espionage".

They were grim days in Caucus. In the month of his declaration of war against the Right, Evatt survived a challenge to his leadership. It was not the only challenge he survived. The old-timers still talk about one Caucus meeting on the leadership. When the time came for the vote to be taken he was in such an emotional state that he leaped on the table demanding that each man should declare himself. The good were to be on his side, the bad on that. He waved his arms and glared at his enemies. In a hard school this was a grim experience.

Here one could introduce a long and dreary list of dates, tracing the great schism in the Labor Party to the famous March 1955 Federal Conference of the A.L.P. which formally and officially ratified the breakdown. However, a month later seven members in the House of Representatives announced themselves as the "Australian Labor Party (Anti-Communist)". "It should be called the Santamaria Group," Evatt said. This very condensed summary of great events in the history of the Labor Party is introduced only as a background to what might be called the finale of the Petrov episode.

We move on to October 1955 for this. The final report of the Royal Commission on Espionage had been presented and it was being debated in the House of Representatives. The Royal Commission's report, running to hundred of pages, stated among other matters in the general conclusions:

All the Petrov Papers are authentic documents.

From these documents alone it plainly appears that for many years the Government of the U.S.S.R. had been using its Embassy at Canberra as a cloak under which to control and operate espionage organizations in Australia.

Evatt spoke for two hours to a crowded House of Representatives on 19th October 1955. Behind him, uncertain and anxious, his own people sat. Flanking him were the bitter members of the Labor breakaway party. In front of him were the Government members. Evatt himself was seething. His speech was not so much a commentary on the report as a discursive review of the entire Petrov affair, and a repetition of his attitude before the Royal Commission.

He attacked from the outset. "After eighteen months of inquiry no spies have been discovered. Not a single prosecution is recommended. . . . It is now clear that the Prime Minister must have known when appointing the Commission that there would be no legal evidence fit to warrant the prosecution of any person, that there was in fact no security

85

ground for the inquiry itself. . . . Furthermore, it is now abundantly clear that the Prime Minister knew many months before April 13, 1954, when he made his melodramatic and coldly calculated announcement to the House, that Petrov's defection was being deliberately organized by security agents under his ministerial control."

The House had expected Evatt to take this line and followed him with no more than the usual amount of advice and interjection. What he said next stupefied the members. When the implications of his words were understood his own people were stony-faced. The Government members laughed, whistled, and stamped.

"I communicated with His Excellency the Foreign Minister for the Soviet Union," Evatt said and you could hear the House gasp. "I pointed out that most of the Russian language documents in the Petrov case were said to be communications from M.V.D. Moscow to Petrov, M.V.D. resident in Australia. I pointed out that the Soviet Union and its officers were undoubtedly in a position to reveal the truth as to the genuineness of the Petrov documents. I duly received a reply sent on behalf of the Minister of Foreign Affairs of the Union of the Soviet Republic, Mr Molotov—"

Members began to laugh. Evatt turned on them angrily.

"Honourable members may laugh," he shouted, "but they have to face some facts tonight. They will not put me off by their organized opposition. They have to listen to this because this is the truth of the affair. The letter to which I have referred informed me that the documents given to the Australian authorities by Petrov 'can only be, as it had been made clear at that time and as it was confirmed later, falsifications fabricated on the instructions of persons interested in the deterioration of the Soviet-Australian relations and in discrediting their political opponents.' "

Shouting and gesticulating above the uproar and the laughter, Evatt said: "I attach grave importance to this letter which shows clearly that the Soviet Government denies the authenticity of the Petrov documents."

He went on and on, but after his disclosure of the Molotov letter the House could scarcely be brought to order; and in this atmosphere the leader of the Opposition became angrier and angrier. He said that early in 1954, shortly before Petrov's defection, the Menzies Government "faced an uncertain position in relation to the following elections." He alleged that the Petrov affair was saved up for the 1954 election, that "the red bogey was to be exhumed again."

White-faced, he said that the Petrov case would rank in history far worse than the Zinoviev letter. He talked about McCarthyism and the tactics of fascism. He talked of attempts to prevent him speaking.

After two hours he sat down.

Coldly, one of his enemies on the flank said, "The most charitable opinion we can form of the Right Honourable gentleman is that he is suffering from strain and overwork."

Later in the debate Menzies spoke. As he went on implacably Evatt interjected with the solitary word "smear" so regularly that it began to sound like a macabre accompaniment. There was no mercy in the attitude and language of the Prime Minister when he ended his speech with these words: "I have referred to those who are charged by the Right Honourable gentleman. Honourable public opinion will acquit them beyond question. But the same honourable public opinion will not acquit the man who made these reckless and villainous charges; nor will it acquit those who have, in this House, authorized those charges, and, by their presence and support, countenanced them. If there is a charge to be made it is this: The leader of the Opposition has, from first to last in this matter, for his own purposes, in his own interests and with the enthusiastic support of every communist in Australia, sought to discredit the judiciary, to subvert the authority of the security organization, to cry down decent and patriotic Australians and to build up the communist fifth column. I am therefore compelled to say that in the name of all those good and honourable men, in the name of public decency, in the name of the safety of Australia, the man on trial in this debate is the Right Honourable gentleman himself."

In October 1955 Federal Parliament was debating the Report of the Royal Commission on Espionage; on 15th November 1955 Menzies was making an election policy speech in the

Canterbury Memorial Hall, Victoria; and on 10th December 1955 the Prime Minister won another election. The losses of the 1954 election were restored. Menzies began his policy speech without any preamble. "It is only eighteen months since you re-elected the Liberal Party and Country Party Government, you may therefore ask why there is a dissolution so soon." He offered two reasons. It was commonsense, he suggested, to have the House of Representatives election on the same day as the Senate election which was required under the Constitution. His second reason was borrowed, cheekily, from Dr Evatt's deputy leader: "The tension and strain now existing in Canberra have made Parliament practically unworkable."

Everybody, of course, knew that Menzies had called an election because in the language politicians understand he had caught his opponents with their pants down.

Policies did not significantly influence the 1955 election. The Molotov letter destroyed the Labor Party's credibility. In politics laughter is a destructive weapon; it ruined the Labor Party hopes in 1955 and destroyed for ever Evatt's chance of becoming Prime Minister. But politicians in both the Labor and the Liberal parties were beginning to recognize in Menzies a rare shrewdness in timing. They recalled his quick and skilful timing in the 1951 double dissolution election, the neatness of the 1954 operation, and the hawk-like strike after the Petrov debate.

After 1955 Evatt was still volcanic, but the eruptions were not so fiery. He led his party to the defeat of 1958, relinquishing the leadership of the Opposition early in 1960 to become Chief Justice of New South Wales. His last long illness was tragic. One wonders whether the seeds of the sickness were always deep in his personality or whether the strains and stresses of his political life led on to the melancholy decline. Some of the symptoms were classic. He was morbidly suspicious and in a man's world he seemed really to be a lonely man. There were signs of a persecution mania and it could be said that he erected in his own mind the delusional structure of a vast plot with himself as the central object. Whether or not this is an accurate diagnosis the last symptoms were acute depression and the twilight of personality. It was very sad.

III

The Terrible Twins

CITIZENS sometimes complain about unparliamentary exchanges between politicians. They say that in so dignified a place as Parliament the members, if they have to insult one another, should be urbane or witty. A nice point, but wit and urbanity are not conferred on all politicians. The average M.P., like the average man, is not quick to select *le mot juste* when provoked. Occasionally, a testy M.P. will strike gold; the Labor M.P., for example, who described a nagging opponent as "sitting on the fence with both ears to the ground". This jewel among mixed metaphors was spontaneous. Its author knew not that inspiration had lightly touched him.

The famous, or notorious (depending on one's political posture) Eddie Ward, for long the darling of East Sydney, was chided for his crude and vulgar interjections. The sewer and the gutter were frequently mentioned by way of comparison. Ward was indifferent to these chidings, which did not do him justice. No member was more assiduous than Ward in his quest for the right phrase, for the right man, at the right time. In his reading he would jot down whatever he thought might be profitably employed in debate. His method was to have half a dozen or so apt observations in his speech notes. He would taunt and lure his destined victim and at the right moment loose the barb. There was the time when a portly member of the Country Party, a rather pompous and turgid chap, offered Ward the opening. Jabbing a finger in the direction of the interjector, Ward snapped: "As stolid as the ox with the vacant stare of centuries on its brow." The Country Party man retired hurt.

Eddie Ward was savage in debate because he looked on politics as part of legitimate warfare between the Classes.

Society for Ward was divided into two irreconcilable groups, the members and supporters of the Labor Party and a mixed lot broadly described as anti-Labor. The most sinister and dangerous of this lot were Capitalists, Profiteers, Warmongers, and Newspaper Proprietors. Their representatives in Parliament sat opposite Ward and they were the creatures of Big Business. Ward regarded them as enemies inside the House and enemies outside. He did not regard Parliament as a debating society where hostilities are only skin deep. Folk unaware of his standards often said that he hit below the belt. Queensberry rules, however, were not in his political code of behaviour. If he had encountered a political opponent wearing a belt around his knees Ward would have kicked him brutally in the shins.

He was an able and tireless debater. Not for him the fine phrase. Fact, fact and punch; fact, fact and punch. That's how he spoke and the words came out of his mouth like bullets. He scarcely paused for breath, never smiled, never tried for theatrical effects. The sameness of his speeches tended to make them monotonous perhaps because of his single-minded dislike of the Enemies of the People. He had the air of an East Sydney Robespierre, a pea-green incorruptible with an Australian accent. In fact, he did not smoke, drink, or use curse words. Meet him away from Canberra and out of the atmosphere of politics and you found a quiet man who would chat innocuously about football and the family. In East Sydney, of course, they adored him.

In the early days of Curtin's ascendancy Eddie Ward and Arthur Calwell were the terrible twins. They buzzed about the rather fastidious John Curtin like gadflies. They were noisy and impatient apostles of socialism. Not intent to pursue the Light on the Hill they wanted to set the hill on fire.

Those were the days when Calwell declared with gusto that he would never be seen wearing a dinner jacket and a black tie, "the uniform of the Capitalist Class".

Ward was an old-hand in the House when Calwell came up to represent Melbourne in 1940. For years Calwell had been waiting, first patiently and then impatiently, for bearded Dr Maloney to die. The doctor had represented the electorate of

Melbourne for more years than one could count. So Calwell was in a hurry when he reached Canberra and he seemed to be in a hurry ever after.

As Minister for Information under Curtin and Chifley, Calwell had a rorty time. He was in head-on conflict with the Press Barons whom he vilified with as much gusto as Ward. But he was more flamboyant than the member for East Sydney. He caught more headlines, was cartooned more often, and was written about more abusively. The wartime censorship dispute between the Government and the Sydney newspapers found Calwell in an authoritarian role. He cheerfully pressed the fight to the point where newspapers were virtually closed down. Editions were seized, Commonwealth police haunted the newspaper offices, and finally the High Court was called on to decide between Calwell and the Press, between security and political censorship. The verdict went to the Press, but Calwell had enjoyed himself immensely. Years later he expressed a mock gratitude to the newspapers for their early assaults. He regarded it all as magnificent publicity.

Calwell was more emotional than Ward about his socialism. He was, indeed, emotional about all his causes. Conscription, for example, aroused him to fury. His fiery conviction brought him into conflict with his leader when Curtin was plodding around Australia from State Division to State Division converting opposition into support for his Militia Bill. Following in his footsteps was an angry Calwell bent on destroying Curtin's design. The last act of this wartime political drama was staged in Federal Parliament. Defying the lightning was dear Maurice Blackburn, a socialist whose principles would not permit him to accept conscription. He was summoned before Headmaster Curtin like a naughty schoolboy, walked in rosy-cheeked and smiling, and walked out smiling, but just as unyielding. Only Calwell stood up in the House to support Blackburn, who persisted to the end and had to leave the Labor Party.

Calwell, in short, was a man of strong opinions and sturdy hates. Early in his Canberra career, however, it was observed by students of the scene that he allowed his emotions to run away with his judgement. He was a man with strong gut reactions. This was to lead him into troubles when he took the leadership of the Federal parliamentary Labor Party.

The records show that Calwell became deputy leader of the Labor Party in June 1951. Not until March 1960 was he able to inform Parliament that he had been elected leader. Thus, for close on a decade he had sat as deputy to the turbulent Dr Evatt. The split in the party and the disappearance of the giants put the mark of leadership on Calwell, but again he had a long wait. Evatt did not willingly surrender the leadership. The electoral defeat of 1958 was insufficient to remove him. For many moons Calwell strode about the lobbies with a lean and hungry look.

The confrontation between Menzies and Calwell was utterly different from the Menzies-Evatt conflict. Calwell and Evatt were not only different in political style and approach; they were dissimilar as men. Physically, emotionally, and mentally they were of different worlds. Under the wide-brimmed hats he affected, and behind the theatrical façade, Calwell was a warm and most likeable man. He also had a sense of fun. A good hater, he was also a strong friend. He could strike attitudes about imperialism and the bloated capitalists, but he was for his country right or wrong. His passion for Australia was glowing. Years of association had developed in Menzies and Calwell a mutual respect which appeared to have matured into liking. Anyhow, if the passages between the two were lively and occasionally terse, enmity was not apparent.

Nevertheless, the great prize was almost thrust into Calwell's hands. How it happened is still recent in memory. The Menzies ear, usually sensitive, had not caught the sounds from the marketplace in the months before the 1961 election. Or was it that the advice of Treasury had been accepted without question? Anyhow, the credit squeeze that was to cure the economy almost killed the Government. When the voters marched on the polling booths in 1961 they were not interested in Arthur Calwell. Their purpose was to register a protest against the Government and it was so potent that for many days Menzies did not know whether he was in or out.

The counting of the last votes gave him a majority of one

on the floor of the House. For Menzies it was a nasty experience; for Calwell, watching the Government seats going down like pins, it was tantalizing and tormenting. In the new Parliament he watched and waited for Menzies to falter or err. Instead, the political mistakes were made by Calwell and the Labor Party, which went to the election of 1963 with the label of the Faceless Men pinned to their organizational leaders.

IV

Interlude: The Place Is Still Odd

FROM the steps of Parliament House you can look down across the lake to the War Memorial and up to the summit of Mount Ainslie which nature surely put there to be crowned by a white Greek temple. All around the central triangle the national capital is growing fast. It has not yet acquired a character of its own. Time, not architectural design, makes a city's personality. Although the city grows and spreads, Parliament House around the King's Hall area is much the same as it was twenty years ago, at the beginning of the Menzies era. On the left of King's Hall, which you can identify by the collection of bad portraits, is the House of Representatives; on the right, the Senate chamber. Running the length of both the House and the Senate are Government lobbies and the Opposition lobbies. The lobbies open on to party rooms and ministerial suites. At the end of the Government lobby on the House side is the Holy of Holies, the prime ministerial suite. This is the centre of power. An ironic observer might liken it to the private apartment in a royal palace. The prime ministerial office opens on to an ante-room which, in turn, leads to the Cabinet Room. In the Menzies era the ante-room gained a certain amount of notoriety. Ostensibly a common room for ministers, it was sneered at by honourable gentlemen out of favour and came to be regarded much as Saint-Simon saw the private apartments of Louis the Fourteenth.

While Parliament is in session all these corridors, rooms, and suites are crowded with members, who seem to be endlessly in motion. Talk is the most conspicuous activity; talk in the House, talk in the party rooms, talk in the suites, at breakfast, lunch, dinner and supper. A parliamentary democracy is somewhat different from a seventeenth century

94

monarchy; but as talk and gossip were the chief occupations in the courts of Europe they remain as significant in the lobbies of Parliament House, Canberra. Courtiers in periwigs were not keener to hear about the King's mood and his newest favourite than the politicians in Canberra are eager to know what's cooking.

It is a very strange experience for the new member. The 1949 Liberal victory carried to Canberra for the first time a very big new crop, for the number of members had been substantially increased by the Chifley Government. Most of the newcomers were barely settled into peacetime callings after the years of war. They were still soldiers, sailors, and pilots. Many of them were starry-eyed about politics and about the Liberal crusade of 1949. In those brave days Menzies was an heroic figure to them. He had led them into battle and on to victory.

A number of the 'forty-niners are still in Parliament. They are considerably older, less starry-eyed, and more worldly about politics. Some are disappointed and embittered. Some are frustrated.

As a group they are not as picturesque as the old brigade that knew Canberra before 1949. The business of government prior to World War II was small potatoes in Canberra. Members had ample time to encourage their oddities and eccentricities.

By way of illustration, we return to the lounge of the Hotel Canberra in those faraway days. A portly and amiable senator has just returned from a formal occasion and he is splendidly turned out in tails and white tie. Awaiting him are two or three of his political colleagues and the senator's wife, who regards him amiably but closely. He is about to accept a drink from his friends when his wife says, "No! not another, you're tight." His wife is adamant and leads the senator away. A few minutes later she returns. "You say he isn't tight," she says, "Well, come along with me." They follow her to the senator's bedroom. He is still in tails and white tie. But he is under the shower and the shower is turned full on.

Growing fast, the place is still odd. The politicians descend from the air on Tuesday morning and disappear into the air on Friday morning. At weekends Parliament House and its approaches are deserted. Out of session it is like a tomb. Misanthropic people still say that the national Parliament should not have been put up in Canberra. They argue that angry city mobs should be close enough to the national Parliament to encourage or intimidate their representatives. They recall that grim night outside the Palais Royal in the heart of French-revolutionary Paris. The sanscullottes had been killing a few aristocrats and were carrying the head of the Princesse de Lamballe on a pike. To encourage the others, they waved the grisly object in front of the windows of the Palais Royal. The Duke of Orleans caught sight of it. Turning languidly to his guests, he remarked, "Ah, there's Lamballe."

The example is extreme, but the critics will argue that Parliament cannot be close to the people when it is surrounded by magpies, crows, and inarticulate fauna. Canberra, however, is growing. In a few years the annual pilgrimage of a few pensioners may be swelled by angry young men from the sprawling suburbs of the national capital. Meanwhile, the M.P. flies home for the weekend. Opening a flower show or selecting a prize melon, he has opportunity to hear the complaints of his constituents.

Does he ever have time to reflect and ask himself why— why did I become a politician? Such meditations perplex the greatest and most successful. "Tiger" Clemenceau, for example, went up to Paderewski, then Prime Minister of Poland, at the Versailles Conference after World War I, and asked, "Why did an artist as gifted as you stoop so low as to become a politician?"

Here people less famous than Clemenceau and Paderewski, have modestly suggested that it makes a man feel important.

A few years ago, in a book gloomily entitled *Can Parliament Survive?*, Christopher Hollis, an English M.P., posed the question, said that it was not simple, and reflected thus: "The disamenities and disadvantages of the life are manifold and manifest. The member of Parliament is at the beck and call of all men day after day from eight o'clock in the morning until twelve o'clock at night. The problems pour in upon him thick and fast without respite and from all directions. He has to give so many decisions that he can never properly give his mind to anything. He has to sacrifice his home life, his recreations and even that cultural background from which we may presume his political convictions derived and without refreshment from which all political convictions must become arid and tasteless and mechanically repetitive. Very few members of Parliament in my experience read many books after their election to Parliament. In return what does he get? In Parliament he finds an unhealthy life full of temptations, all the frustration of endless hours of bobbing up and down to catch the Speaker's eye in order in the end to mumble for a quarter of an hour to empty benches. . . . He has to play his part in the party game, much of which the keenest of politicians must with all the will in the world often feel to be a dreary and childish farce. A few persons of a certain temperament prefer to live their lives and to do their talking thus in the public gaze, but to the normal man it is an unnatural life —the life of a man living continually on his nerves."

"What is it that causes anyone to lead such a life?" sorrowfully asks Christopher Hollis. The answers he offers discuss the love of power ("the number of politicians who have any share in shaping the destiny of nations is very small") and an intense desire for success, "that extra little ounce of ambition that is not quite sane".

We are left with the thought that politicians are not all of a piece, any more than other people. Every sort of motive, he says, from the highest ideal of disinterested service to the lowest and most sordid self-seeking, leads men to politics.

Placed somewhat lower than angels they inhabit a territory above the infernal regions. We are asked to be content with this broad generalization.

Part Four

PORTRAIT OF THE ARTIST

I

The Man

For eighteen years Robert Gordon Menzies was Prime Minister and for six years leader of the Opposition. As far back as 30th November 1954 he set a new record of seven years and 106 days. The statisticians on his staff had worked out the survey. Hughes ran second with seven years and 105 days, Lyons third with seven years and 93 days. After 30th November 1954, what point was there in keeping a tally? It went on and on, making a grand total of eighteen years and a bit by the time the seventy-one-year-old Menzies, on 20th January 1966, announced his resignation.

"I have been Prime Minister for a total of over eighteen years," he said. "Two of these years were in the war period. Sixteen have been consecutive since 1949. Prior to 1949, I led the Opposition for six years, during a period in which we were heavily outnumbered, and my own responsibility and labours were both intense and sustained."

Since he became leader of the Opposition at the end of 1943 he had been responsible for the conduct of eight general elections and two separate Senate elections. "I am tired; my pace has slowed down," he said. "The thought of going through another election campaign would depress me."

The November 1964 Senate campaign had tired him. "The strain of election campaigns is something that the onlooker cannot be expected fully to understand," he said. For an athlete in peak form an election campaign in Australia would be tiring. Menzies was close on seventy. He often said he had the constitution of a horse, but even horses break down. Before the actual campaign begins, preparation and planning, unknown to the public, must take place. In this the Prime Minister is very much involved. There is much to be done on the Cabinet level and a policy speech has to be written. Then, after the opening night of the campaign, the party leader has to survive two, sometimes three weeks of madness—meeting after meeting, and flight after flight, to Queensland, to Western Australia, to every State. Into this tight schedule he has to fit the business of government, tactical conferences, radio programmes, and in these days, television programmes, which require long and careful preparation.

By the time the 1964 Senate campaign came up Menzies had little enthusiasm for taking the road again. After a week he was crotchety and weary and nobody knew better than Menzies that bad temper and good judgement do not go together.

As 1965 wore on shrewd observers tipped that Menzies was turning over in his mind the big decision. It was important and unusual because, in politics, a man does not often go out of office under his own steam. But he was conscious of an accumulating "wear and tear". Speech-making had become a burden. That, indeed, was obvious.

So, on 20th January 1966, when he talked to the Canberra Press Gallery, everything had been neatly sorted out in his mind, and he sat quietly talking about a quarter of a century, a long time to be on stage in a star role. He was mellow and relaxed.

He was not always mellow and relaxed. You cannot run a business so public and controversial as the government of the Commonwealth of Australia without annoying somebody. A nonentity might survive without making enemies, but not for eighteen years. Anyhow, a man of Menzies' make-up could not have run a country pub without antagonizing some of his customers.

"He had been presented often as an authoritarian figure who left his Cabinet very little opportunity to make a contribution to the matters coming before it," said Prime Minister

Harold Holt when Parliament was saying nice things about the departed Menzies. This, said Harold Holt, was a false picture. He spoke of "other aspects of this mythology—an aloofness of manner and a coolness of temperament. . . . Those of us who were close to him know what a warm, friendly, charming companion the right honourable gentleman is to all who come intimately into contact with him."

Some who did not come intimately into contact with Menzies had different views. The names they called him, however, were, usually, not rude. Politely he was Sir Robert, after the night of the Thistle. Traditionally, he was addressed as "Prime Minister", or "P.M." for short, by his colleagues. Informally, one rarely heard him addressed as "Bob". The very bold, or one or two of the pre-1943 "loyalists", might say Bob. Fadden and a few others spoke of the Big Fella. In the Press Gallery it was Ming, a diminutive of Ming the Merciless, a comic strip character of singular ferocity and a play on the tribal pronunciation of his name. The waterside workers christened him Pig-Iron Bob but he wore that as a badge of honour. Inside Canberra few referred to him as the Boss; more often than not it was Ming. Menzies himself, of course, did not encourage familiarity.

There is a duality in most political leaders, a public and a private self. In Menzies the public self worked overtime. Thirty-seven years of parliamentary life, twenty-six of them as a minister or as Prime Minister, had given him little if any, private life as most people know it. To see Menzies put on his public self was an extraordinary spectacle. Towards the end of his term as Prime Minister age was showing in his face and movements. Sitting alone he could look authoritatively like a seventy-year-old grandfather. He could be stoop-shouldered, his thoughts a world away, his hands flat on his knees.

Suddenly, the bells ring. He stirs himself, he slowly stands up, he issues to himself some mysterious command, the figure seems to grow larger, the face takes on the look of command, and with a paper under his arm, he moves majestically into the lobby, for the world to see. And what the world saw was, in spite of Harold Holt's interpretation, an authoritarian, aloof figure. The performance could not have been achieved by a man physically small. The stature, the massive head, and the sheer bulk were splendid raw material to be used by a master of presentation.

It is not to be imagined, however, that behind the façade, masterful and remote, lurked a private self as sweet as a new-born baby. The real Menzies, as exposed in his younger days, was hardly tender. Perhaps, he did not, like George Curzon, say "I am a very superior person", but he was addicted to the vice of not suffering fools gladly. Thus, to assume the purple of authority may not have been wholly against the grain.

The progress from the Prime Minister's office to the table in the House was stately and impressive, without any theatrical aids such as red carpets, trumpets, or page boys. The presence was sufficient. Members did not walk nonchalantly up to him, button-hole him, or slap him on the back. They didn't call out greetings. They inclined to step aside. Sometimes he would nod and smile. He arrived at the table in time for Mr Speaker to say prayers and then awaited the daily questioning. Sometimes he gazed into space, sometimes lightly rested his head on the palm of his hand, sometimes doodled. He disposed of the questions addressed to him briefly and urbanely. After question time, if nothing was on the paper requiring his presence, he would move slowly from the House back to his office.

Rarely did he stroll into the party room to chat with the back-benchers. One did not see him breasting the parliamentary bar. His habit was to take his meals at the Lodge. The place for pre-lunch or pre-dinner drinks was the exclusive ante-room adjoining the Prime Minister's office. So back-benchers saw little of him socially. Some of them complained that they saw little of him in any role. If these complaints reached him, they did not appear to disturb him.

At his last Press Conference he was asked what he would miss most as an ex-Prime Minister.

"Oh, I don't know," he replied. "You know there is a great theory in the world that people like myself who become Prime Minister go around blowing out their bags and feeling a great sense of power. I have never had any feeling of that kind."

Well, he may not have felt power inside himself; many of those about him felt it. It was rarely necessary for him to make long disapproving speeches to those who had offended. A look was sufficient, a frown was devastating. At the opposite end of the scale, a nod or a wink cured cases of acute depression. His moods were closely studied. If he came into a meeting with a clear brow the company relaxed; when he strode in with a dark look the company was tense.

Those huge, black eyebrows told a story. A cultivated growth, they appeared to be stuck on. They gave the face a mephistophelian look. He manipulated them to register surprise, incredulity, appreciation. Menace was not their function. The furrow above his nose was a surer sign of impatience; his mouth slanted tightly when his mood was dark. His eyes were used with dramatic effect. Whenever he dispensed charm he directed a quite brilliant glitter upon his subject. Laughter was rarely employed, certainly not belly laughter. But there was ample room on the face to display mood, although it was all done as if by command from some secret source. Face and head were constructed on monumental lines—a combination ruling out mercurial changes of expression. The technique was slow motion.

When you walk up the broad flight of steps leading to King's Hall you confront Ivor Hele's portrait of Robert Gordon Menzies. The likeness is superficial, in accordance with some curious convention that the portraits in King's Hall must provide no clue to the personalities of the men who sit for them. Indeed, the tourists who wander around King's Hall might know a little more about Menzies if the *Time* cover portrait by Dobell greeted them at the top of the steps. It is a brooding, sour interpretation, but it does try to look beneath the skin.

He disliked being caught unprepared by peripatetic photographers. He was reluctant to sit for a studio photograph. Although such reservations are not uncommon, Menzies did not like to be caught unprepared for anything. How much his on-guard posture was native to him or how much it owed to the throat-cutting days of 1939 and 1941, who can say? After his triumphal return in 1949 he was probably a more suspicious mortal. One suspects that he said aloud, as he read his Shakespeare, "such men are dangerous."

It would be whimsical to see Menzies painted *à la Louis Quatorze* with a periwig framing that dominating face. Menzies in the setting of Louis the Fourteenth would not have been too utterly fantastic to those imaginative fellows in Canberra who saw the Prime Minister in his sunny years as a monarch surrounded by acquiescent and subservient courtiers. Parliament House is no Versailles and King's Hall would be no fitting stage for the Sun King. The ante-room adjoining the Prime Minister's office has no seventeenth century glitter. But, alas, there will always be flatterers and men susceptible to flattery. In this context some who did not idolize Menzies saw him and those with the right of entry.

He did not rule as long as Louis the Fourteenth, but his reign was very long by Australian political standards. Inevitably, the closing years irked the young, and some of the older members of the party much as the rigidity and tedium of the French court in the last years of the old King exasperated everybody except the elderly clique clinging to special privileges like handing the King his shirt. To think of that gallery when walking in Canberra's parliamentary lobbies might seem extravagantly inappropriate. But these lobbies, unglamorous, are corridors of power in this country, and those who walk the corridors of power, whether they wear a periwig or an Australian suit, don't change much in their methods. They perform in a more recognizable manner when the man at the top is the master, as well as appearing to be. He doesn't need to hand out *lettres de cachet*. There are other roads to exile.

Striding about London when the bombs were falling, Menzies was as tough and durable as he sometimes looked. Election platforms, though less dangerous than bomb-strewn streets, can daunt the timid. Back in the 'forties, while Menzies was still Pig-Iron Bob and Public Enemy No. 1 to the Communist Party, he went to a meeting at the Maccabean Hall in East Sydney that excelled most meetings before or since in its violence. It became a riot rather than an election meeting. As Menzies stood up to speak the stacked meeting erupted.

Men stood, stamped, shouted, screamed. They waved banners, they threw banners. "Pig-Iron, Pig-Iron, Pig-Iron," they chanted. Then they started to throw pig-iron. The platform became dangerous. Menzies stood and talked but nobody heard him. The uproar was hideous. When Menzies stood unruffled and disdainful, they became ugly and the police took a hand. One man was lifted bodily from the mob and carted off. The seething floor of the hall was riotous. On stage Menzies stood with the standing group of his supporters. He refused to budge or to end the meeting. The mob yelled, howled, and threw things. The policemen grabbed the more violent ones. It went on and on and the police vans were overflowing.

Menzies declined to leave by a side door. "I came in the front way and I am going out the front way," he said. And down he stalked while they howled and stamped. It was quite a night.

"How did you get the name Pig-Iron Bob?" Menzies was asked at a meeting in Victoria during 1960.

The Prime Minister replied in the manner that could always be guaranteed to infuriate his opponents.

"I was given the name by the Communists," he said. "You see, the Communist-led waterside workers at Port Kembla were refusing to load a ship for Japan at a time when we were at peace with that country. They undertook to take charge of the foreign policy of this country. . . . So I went down to Port Kembla. I didn't talk to them on the long-distance telephone, I went down and met them on the spot; and I told them they were going back to work because we were in charge of the government of the country. And they went back to work. Since then I have honourably borne this title."

The coalminers also got to know him well. They were striking for a shorter working week. It was 1940 and World War II had begun. So Menzies decided to front the miners. He arranged to speak to them at the Kurri Kurri picture theatre. About three thousand miners expressed themselves pointedly by marching off to their own meeting at the local sports ground. A few friendly people remained to hear Menzies, who then strode off to the sports ground. The astonished miners saw the unmistakable and detested figure and couldn't believe their eyes. He waited calmly and patiently for the union leaders to finish their speeches, then heard the men debate a motion that he should be heard. They heard him, they heckled him, and some of them even admired him, because it was extraordinary to see and hear one man against three thousand. Yes, he was a tough customer in those days.

In the tentative period between 1945 and 1949 a bright public relations adviser, a fleeting and temporary figure, suggested that Menzies might find the common touch by occasionally appearing in city bars to astonish the multitude as a kind of beer-drinking democrat. The experiment, in which Menzies reluctantly participated, was not successful. It was a silly idea, anyhow.

Later, as Prime Minister again, Menzies was somewhat allergic to public relations gimmickry. Yet, unrehearsed, unnoticed, and not reported, he could sometimes do things that would have made P.R. men swoon with delight. For example, he was in Brisbane to address a Law Convention. Lennon's Hotel was full of judges, men learned in the law, and Menzies. It was about lunch time on Saturday. The Prime Minister's press secretary met an old friend and they decided to look for a Queensland mud-crab lunch. "But first I must see if the old man wants me," said the press secretary. Menzies was alone in his room. "I'll walk with you," he said. Leaving the hotel crowded with distinguished lawyers, many of whom he knew well, the Prime Minister accompanied the mud-crab explorers until they found a small, scrubby fish-shop with a notice in the window tersely announcing: "Mud Crab".

"May I join you?" asked Menzies. He edged into a tiny cubicle with scarcely room to breathe, and toyed with prawns while the other two fell upon the mud crab. Two plump, giggling waitresses lined up, presented Menzies with grubby pieces of paper and asked for autographs, which they got. Then the proprietor sidled up, a swarthy little Maltese, who somehow squeezed into the cubicle and sat by Menzies. He at once related his family history and asked the Prime Minister if he could help. How? "It is my brother in Malta. He would like to come here." Menzies took some notes. The Maltese beamed. The waitresses giggled. A trifle flushed after being crowded into so minute an area, Menzies moved into Adelaide Street, said goodbye to his two luncheon companions, and walked back towards his hotel.

The press secretary gazed after him in astonishment and despair. "In there eating prawns, signing autographs, talking to that fish merchant—and not a bloody photographer for miles. Come and have a drink. I need one."

In the mood, he had a nice feeling for the comic. There was an occasion in Sydney that left the onlookers dazed and speechless. Menzies was leaving a finance dinner attended by about five hundred well-to-do Sydney businessmen, not a particularly humorous lot. As the door of a large lift opened to convey Menzies to the ground floor, he observed Bruce Graham, the Liberal M.P. For Graham he had an affection and would address him as "Claverh-o-o-se", after the Earl of Claverhouse and Viscount Dundee, titles of noble vintage among the Grahams.

Menzies addressed Graham sternly: "Claverhouse, sing the song!"

"Here, sir?"

"Here and now!"

So, as the lift descended and surrounded by startled guests, Graham sang a verse and the chorus of "The Bonnets of Bonnie Dundee":

> *To the Lords of Convention 'twas Claver'se who spoke:*
> *"Ere the King's crown shall fall there are crowns to be*
> *   broke;*
> *So let each Cavalier who loves honour and me,*
> *Come follow the bonnet of Bonny Dundee.*
>
> *"Come fill up my cup, come fill up my can,*
> *Come saddle your horses, and call up your men;*
> *Come open the West Port, and let me gang free,*
> *And it's room for the bonnets of Bonny Dundee!"*

The great man listened courteously, said "Good evening, Claverhouse," and strode away into the night leaving behind a pop-eyed audience.

He had a talent for writing light verse, not surprising in a man with his feeling for the word. It is said that actress Katharine Hepburn, in Canberra in 1955, called him "a wicked man" after reading his version of the *Merchant of Venice* court scene. Menzies had ventured lightly to put Shakespeare right in his law. On other occasions, usually festive, he would write down a few barbed lines. It was not always a one-way traffic. Others fired arrows back. One little set of rhymes began with, "Robert the King was hard to know. . . ."

> *Robert the King was hard to know,*
> *When he died and went below*
> *Historians couldn't say for sure*
> *Whether his memory would endure.*
>
> *Lesser folk could not hob-nob*
> *With Robert the King or call him Bob.*
> *"Hail, Caesar!" was the better line*
> *And almost made him feel divine.*
>
> *Though this enlarged his royal bliss*
> *It wasn't good analysis,*
> *For underneath the kingly splendour*
> *The man was really very tender.*
>
> *They put a crown upon his head*
> *And though he wore it into bed,*
> *He sometimes said as he sadly sat,*
> *"It's not a crown, it's an old felt hat!"*

In private he was an excellent mime and could take off people neatly. He was an amiable and entertaining host, a role he enjoyed. The dinner table suited him perfectly. Inside a cloud of cigar smoke, he would talk copiously. These occasions were revealing and disclosed his middle-class attitudes. He was no highbrow, a type he regarded suspiciously. He was not an intellectual, as the word is used to describe certain learned, erudite gentlemen. Aesthetically, he was a square. A friend of the artist Harold Herbert, he liked paintings in which trees, mountains, skies could be recognized. He liked portraits to represent the sitter literally. Such names as Picasso distressed him. Abstract art conveyed no message to him. His reading was extensive, but one could not imagine him spending a long weekend with James Joyce. Music was not a significant adventure in his life. One day a very distinguished 'cellist, a man well and warmly known to Menzies, called on him at the Lodge. The Prime Minister had done this musician a service and the question was how to thank Menzies. The matter was resolved when the 'cellist produced his precious instrument, sat himself down, and poured into the surprised ears of the Prime Minister one long movement from a 'cello concerto. The scene was remarkable, one lone 'cellist and one lone Prime Minister in a big room.

His felt hats and his double-breasted suits became almost as well-known as his eyebrows. This was not a sartorial affectation. He had little dress sense and was perhaps self-conscious about his figure. Yet it was a very imposing figure. In tails and white tie and adorned with his ribbons etc., he looked splendid. He probably did not feel very comfortable. Where Churchill liked dressing up, Menzies liked dressing down. This reticence was broken down with the years. He had to put on so many academic hats, not to mention the odd skull cap, and in due course the green robes and grand hat of the Thistle, that the ultimate admiral's garb of the Lord Warden presented no insuperable problems.

Peculiarities about dress were a pointer to his sensitivity. He was not only sensitive to criticism; he was sensitive to mood and atmosphere. His intuitions were so keen that he seemed almost able to read a man's thoughts. Perception so sharp was an asset in Parliament and at public meetings. The mood of an audience was conveyed to him as if by a ray. A lifetime of public speaking could not deaden the reaction of his nerves to a great occasion. Indeed, the confident, bold exterior protected, one surmises, a shy inner self—an apparent contradiction not rare among men.

Imperial England he loved. This abiding affection may have been rooted in his understanding of and pride in British history and political institutions. He wrote sensitively and understandingly about the feel of England. His regard for the grand circle of eighteenth century English statesmen was real and vivid, and in his own time he enjoyed the association with the men at the head of English affairs. He said time and again that Australia would always be his home and often he said emphatically "no" to newspapermen who asked whether he fancied retiring to the House of Lords. Yet London was always alluring. Sometimes he looked an authentic part of the scene. Robed in his Thistle green, he sat for a photograph like some massive figure plucked out of Tudor England. He was familiar with Downing Street and at home in the Savoy. In the pavilion at Lord's he paused one day and said dramatically, "This is the cathedral of cricket." At an English dinner table with a lighted cigar, and a glass of old brandy at his elbow, he was expansive and content.

His affection for England kindled the words of his tribute on the occasion of the State funeral of Sir Winston Churchill on 30th January 1965. "As I end my talk to you from the crypt of St Paul's," he said, "with its reminders of Nelson and Wellington, those marvellous defenders of long ago, the body of Winston Churchill goes in procession through the streets of London; *his* London, *our* London, this most historic city, this ancient home of freedom, this place through which, in the very devastation and fire of war, *his* voice rang with courage, and defiance and hope, and rugged confidence. His body will be carried on the Thames, a river full of history. With one heart we all feel, with one mind we all acknowledge that it will never have borne a more precious burden, or been enriched by more splendid memories."

II

The Politician

OPPONENTS tried to provoke him by saying sneeringly that he belonged to the eighteenth century. This amiable taunt acknowledged his respect for the great men of the Pitt era; a closer study of his thinking would have been far more rewarding to politicians who believed they had found a political philosophy when they repeated one or two Platform clichés. At what point in his political education did Menzies look into the mind of Edmund Burke, that Irishman who, in a company of giants, was acclaimed as the greatest of English orators, measured by the immediate effect of his impassioned speaking and the durability of his political thinking?

For Menzies to have sought enlightenment in Edmund Burke would not have been a novel exercise. The English conservatives, in times of defeat, look back to the sources of their belief. They did this after the defeat of 1945. The re-thinking in this period was a prelude to their return to power. "Modern Conservatism," they wrote, "would not have received the impetus, which has brought us to our present position, were it not that this period has been enlivened by contributions made by the successors of Bolingbroke, Pitt, Burke, and Disraeli, who inspire the pedestrian task of policy-making with a philosophy. . . . A party founded upon an attitude built up from the spiritual truths and the continuous experience of history should never date, provided that its principles are interpreted in the modern idiom: Disraeli did not found a new Party. He restated the truths of Bolingbroke and Burke for his age."

When Menzies sat down to write a draft for the Objectives of the Liberal Party of Australia he had, indeed, "to inspire the pedestrian task of policy-making with a philosophy". Put another way, he had to settle upon a set of political principles. Few among those who went to Canberra and Albury at his invitation had the training, the reading, or the flair to undertake this task. They could talk enthusiastically about private enterprise and the rights of the individual which they believed were menaced by socialism. They could not define a set of political principles. You don't conjure up political principles out of the thin air, you look for them in the record of man's political history and experience; and where, for Menzies, was a better place to begin than in the Parliament that evolved our political institutions?

One has only to read Edmund Burke to know that Menzies was influenced by him. One has only to listen to Menzies to be even more certain. So let us, by way of a diversion, return to the eighteenth century for a moment. Sometimes, the century of William Pitt, Edmund Burke and Charles James Fox is a million light-years away from us; at other times it is only yesterday. Men and women of the second half of the twentieth century who bitterly know the evil of arbitrary power might have listened to Burke had they heard him in the House of Commons. His periods would have wearied them, but perhaps not his sentiments.

George III was young and ambitious when Burke entered public life in 1765 as the member for Wendover. The thirty-six-year-old Burke was soon to take a leading part in the first of the great causes for which he fought—the freedom of the House of Commons against the designs of the King. George III thought he had the ability and undoubtedly he had the will to run England and its Empire. His two predecessors, tied to Hanover, had been content to allow men of the singular talents of Walpole and Chatham to direct the nation. The third George placed his own dull-witted creatures in office, reserving real power to himself. A combination of corruption and stupidity lost an empire, but gained for Parliament the right, never after challenged, to govern. In this struggle Burke was a champion of Parliament.

The second great cause he fought was for the American colonies against the claim of George's ministers to tax them directly. His third and most far-reaching political battle was against the French Revolution and "the spirit of atheistical Jacobinism".

In all these conflicts—and in his attitudes towards India—we see the shaping of principles which influenced not only his own times but the subsequent history of English politics. He did not elaborate any system, and turned his mind away from the discussion of purely theoretical issues. He argued that in practical politics, the guiding star of statesmanship is expediency, not legal or abstract right. Burke used the word "expediency" not in its modern "take-the-easy-way-out" sense. His stand on the American colonies illustrates the point; legal rights should be exercised by an entire regard for liberty and the spirit of England's own Constitution. He contended also, in formulating his second principle of action, that in the quest for what is expedient and right, the statesman must be guided by circumstances, the most important being the temper and character of the people for whom he legislates. Finally, he declared that the safest guide to action is experience; "the past illumines the future."

In the advocacy of his political principles, Burke was an eloquent defender of the party system when it was fashionable to decry party as "faction". He saw the party system as an indispensable instrument of practical statesmanship. "Party," he said, "is a body of men united for promoting by their joint endeavours the national interest upon some particular principle in which they are all agreed."

For Burke, above all, politics had to be interpreted in terms of men, not systems, not theories. The clarity of his thinking in this context was shown in his hostility to Warren Hastings. Chatham could win an empire—the Indian empire; but how was he to govern people who had never known any other rule than an absolute despotism? Burke said that the Government had allowed despotism to pass to a trading company. His indignation shook the walls of Westminster.

The Burke who interests us most is the crusader against the French Revolution. In his great speeches on this topic he defined an attitude that has enormously influenced conservative political thinking down to our own times. Indeed, Burke on the French Revolution is very modern to a generation familiar with Hitler and Stalin.

"Arbitrary power," said Burke, "is a thing which neither any man can hold nor any man can give." It must be remembered, however, that he was a child of the English Revolution of 1688, as he was a friend of the American revolution. He did not oppose the French Revolution because it was a revolt against legitimate authority or a radical reconstruction of the machinery of State. He damned the French Revolution as the product of an abstract philosophy false to the fundamental facts of man's moral and political nature. Force, he said, cannot justify a man renouncing his liberty or (as he saw it in the eighteenth century) his responsibility to God. His foe was arbitrary power.

In his *Reflections on the French Revolution* he developed his concept of the individual as the product of society, born to an inheritance of rights and reciprocal duties. These were embodied in law and established by usage. "Revolution," he declared, "will be judged by the degree in which it preserves as well as destroys and by what it substitutes for what it takes away."

With this background in mind, let us look in on the House of Commons on 9th February 1790. The French Revolution is still young. The King's head is still on his shoulders. His queen is alive and, considering all things, not yet heart-broken. The Terror has not begun. In the London of these years, in the elegant squares and the aristocratic clubs, men of sensibility and of the Whig persuasion see in the events in France the dawn of a new age of liberty. This group, headed by the brilliant, careless, beloved Charles James Fox, does not include their admired friend, the austere and gloomy Edmund Burke.

February 9 was an acrimonious night in the House of Commons. They were debating the Army estimates when Burke rose to make the first of his many historic speeches on the French Revolution. He denounced it with all his fire, passion, and eloquence. He then moved on to a brilliant and penetrating comparison between the happenings in France and the English revolution of 1688.

"It is to be lamented," he said, "that this strange thing called a revolution in France should be compared with the glorious event commonly called the revolution in England. In truth, the circumstances of our revolution, as it is called, and that of France, are just the reverse of each other in almost every particular, and in the whole spirit of the transaction.

"What we did was, in truth and substance, not a revolution made, but prevented. We took solid securities; we settled doubtful questions; we corrected anomalies in our laws. In the stable, fundamental parts of our Constitution we made no revolution; no, nor any alteration at all. We did not impair the monarchy. The nation kept the same ranks, the same subordinations, the same franchises, the same order in the law, the revenue, and the magistracy—the same Lords, the same Commons, the same corporations, the same electors. The Church was not impaired. . . ."

An excited Commons heard his conclusion. "Was little done, then, because a revolution was not made in the Constitution? No. Everything was done, because we commenced with reparation, not ruin."

Charles James Fox disagreed with his distinguished friend and colleague. "If a general destruction of the ancient Constitution has taken place in France, it was because the whole system was radically hostile to liberty, and that every part of it breathed the direful spirit of despotism."

Richard Brinsley Sheridan, joining with Fox, threw back at Burke his own words. "Are the mad outrages of a mob," he said, "an adequate ground for branding the National Assembly with the stigma of being a bloody, ferocious, and tyrannical democracy?"

The debate divided the nation as well as the Parliament. On 6th May 1791 the Commons, its emotions inflamed by the conflict between Burke and Fox, witnessed one of the most moving and historic of scenes, a parting that changed the course of political affairs. In another bitter attack on the French Revolution, Burke said that although he had differed on many occasions from Mr Fox, there had been no loss of friendship. "But," he went on, "there is something in the accursed French Constitution that envenoms everything."

"There is no loss of friendship," Fox interjected emotionally.

"There is," retorted Burke, "I know the price of my conduct. I have done my duty. Our friendship is at an end."

The Commons, silent, saw Fox in tears. This master of words could summon no words for a few minutes. Then he moved the whole assembly with an impassioned plea to Burke, who made no answer. A great friendship and political association had ended, and, with it, a political era.

Back in twentieth century Australia, it is instructive to glance at the expression and the political principles, very largely the language and thoughts of Menzies, in the objectives of the Liberal Party of Australia as accepted by the Canberra Conference in 1944, and in the concise statement of beliefs entirely in the language of Menzies, entitled *We Believe*, which is handed to most new branch members of the party.

In his opening speech at the Canberra Conference, Menzies said that there was no useful place in Australia for a party of negation. He then outlined what he regarded as "our ultimate objectives". There were trace elements of Burke in these sentences:

A country in which there is free thought and free speech and free association for all except the enemies of freedom. . . .

A country in which no consideration of wealth and privilege will determine the education of either child or man, who shall each be fully trained in his own powers. . . .

A country in which values will have been so corrected that the greatest rewards go to those who perform the truest services to the people. . . .

A country in which Parliament controls the Executive and the Law controls all.

Phrases in *We Believe* carry a similar rhythm and association of ideas: "We believe that it is the supreme function of government to assist in the development of personality; that today's dogma may turn out to be tomorrow's error; and that, in consequence, the interests of all legitimate minorities must be protected. . . . We believe that rights connote duties. . . .

We believe that national financial and economic power and policy are not to be designed to control men's lives, but to create a climate in which men may be enabled to work out their own salvation in their own way."

There is also strong traditional association in Menzies' attitude to the monarchy. Delivering the first Smuts Memorial Lecture at the University of Cambridge in 1960 he asked: "Are we the Queen's men and women because, as the fact is, we love and respect her? Or because, out of long experience, we find in the monarchy as such a focal point, unmarred by political controversy, for our national tradition, consciousness, and ambition?" He went on to say that "we British people . . . have a deep instinct for the monarchy. . . . The Georgian era provided some evidence that the people of Britain thought it a better thing to have an indifferent or incompetent King (or even Regent) than no king at all."

"Allegiance to the Crown," he said, "will remain, intangible, not susceptible of legal definition, the most profound of all the unifying influences for the Crown dominions."

At his final press conference in Canberra he was asked what he saw as his most lasting achievement. "On the political side, I think I look back with most satisfaction on two things," he replied, "the creation in 1944 of the Liberal Party out of about fourteen fragments, and this was a highly individual task; and the fruitful and constant alliance with the Country Party in the Federal Parliament."

The final accounting will almost certainly put the formation of the Liberal Party at the head of his achievements. His resolve to achieve what appeared impossible was strengthened by his experiences in his first term as Prime Minister. He told a State Liberal Conference in Hobart in 1960 that "in disunity we found our greatest disaster, and in unity we found our greatest and most continuous success." He reminded his Liberal audience that in the dying days of the United Australia Party a crop of different organizations had sprung up in Australia, "all of them professing, more or less, our own point of view". Disunity of that kind, he said, was one of the reasons for defeat. He showed how disunity in its ranks wrecked the

Bruce-Page Government and how the Scullin Labor Government had fallen to pieces. "Every time there is disunity," he said, "disaster may be looked for. Every time there is unity, victory is three parts achieved."

Making a party was not easy, nor was winning an election with a new party. At first, sceptics said that the Liberal Party was the old gang masquerading under a different name. The fact was that most of the old gang (outside the parliamentary party) had been dropped, but the hard work of building branches across the continent took time. More important was electoral opinion. What are called the swing voters had not, by 1946, abandoned the Chifley Government. The run from the A.L.P. began with Chifley's declaration of war on the private banks. This incredible political mistake so frightened the business community that the refrain "You can't win with Menzies" was heard infrequently.

The Liberal Party organization and Menzies mounted a powerful campaign for the 1949 Federal election and endorsed an enthusiastic and able team of candidates. They went into battle snorting like war-horses. Menzies himself worked lovingly on his policy speech. He said at the outset what he repeated at later elections, that a policy speech was not just a list of promises, but "a high and real conflict of principles". In comparison with the policy speeches of the 'fifties that of 1949 was crowded with undertakings. This, of course, was because an Opposition was seeking office after years in exile. It required a comprehensive policy programme. Nevertheless, a choice in beliefs was presented.

"This is our great year of decision," said Menzies. "Are we for the Socialist State, with its subordination of the individual to the universal officialdom of government, or are we for the current British faith that governments are the servants of the people, a faith which has given fire and quality and direction to the whole of our history for six hundred years?"

It was rhetorical stuff, spoken with great gusto by Menzies. Earthy voters, however, reacted more cheerfully when he said that he would repeal the Bank Nationalization Act and that he proposed legislation to amend the Constitution, "by making it impossible for such socialist legislation to be passed in future without your approval given at a referendum."

And so, at the end of 1949, Robert Gordon Menzies, who had constructed a new party, was Prime Minister again, the head of a coalition. The leadership had been restored to him in full. Could he retain it? Some of his closest colleagues will tell you that Menzies learned so much in those lean Opposition years that he was a different man after 1949. Others, of course, will dispute this. One short story may help us to reach a conclusion. He offered an important portfolio to a man who in the years of conflict had opposed him. Looking reflectively across the green lawns in front of Parliament House, the minister-to-be spoke of the yesterdays. Menzies put a hand lightly on his shoulder. "We all grow up sometime," he said, which may or may not have been a confession as well as a pardon.

From 1949 until his retirement Menzies was a strong party leader, strong in the sense that he was the No. 1 man and expected 100 per cent backing for party decisions. Nearly always he got the backing, but not always with love! As his hair became whiter he took on the appearance of a headmaster. Bad boys were not hoisted for a flogging but they had the feeling they were standing in a corner with backs to the class. Bad boys who talked back drew nasty pictures about the Head. He ignored them. He never made prefects of them. With others, he could be the Head who made embarrassingly cutting remarks.

But a political leader must be the Boss. He may be liked, respected, or barely tolerated. He must be the Boss. Curtin and Chifley, in their time, were the masters of their party. One wonders whether Evatt, for all his talent, was the Head-master. It may be said, therefore, that Menzies the politician had the qualities of leadership, "to which," the bad boys say, "he joined the defects of personality."

One of the most exacting tests of his leadership followed the Federal election of 1961, which was run so close that for some days Menzies did not know whether he was in or out of office. In the early and mid-'fifties the Prime Minister had permitted heavy and unpopular restraints to curb inflation and had survived at the polls. Towards the end of 1960 the Government decided to quell an inflationary boom that had swollen alarmingly. The medicine was prescribed in the November 1960 economic measures—the detested Credit Squeeze. So harsh was the squeeze that the patient breathed with difficulty. The result was not to restore a normal state of affairs but to push up unemployment figures to the point where they became a political menace to the Government.

Menzies, however, went to the country unrepentent. For once his sense of smell had deserted him. To a sullen and morose electorate he said, in the second paragraph of his policy speech, "I do not propose to put before you a long list of promises. . . . We offer you good government," etc. etc. He did talk about the boom and the squeeze, but said that the last survivor of the emergency measures, the restrictions on Bank Credit, had been eliminated "two weeks ago".

Two weeks before the opening of an election campaign was not a nice piece of timing. Voters forgive and forget if the politicians allow them time enough. Although Menzies knew this, he could not talk the electors out of their resentment in one short campaign. Twenty-four hours after the counting of votes began the final state of the parties was unpredictable.

Menzies, familiar since 1949 with victory, was unexpectedly philosophical. He chatted affably to a press conference while the outcome was still obscure. "If we are out, we are out. . . . If we are, all I can say is that the people of Australia have given me their confidence for a long time and, therefore, I have no personal grievance, none at all. . . . I suppose that by the end of the week we will know what the results are. I feel rather like King Charles, you know, who apologized for being such an unconscionable time a-dying."

Reminiscent, he said it had been his fifteenth election. "And I thought I knew every noise an election campaign made and could form a pretty rough idea as to whether the tide was coming in or out." Then, cheerfully, "I'm a good sleeper. That's why I remain outside the lunatic asylum."

The long-drawn-out suspense ended when the last few votes gave the Queensland seat of Moreton to the Government, a survival by one. Menzies was sitting in the ante-room of his suite in Parliament House when the news was brought to him. He had been discussing possible moves if the result had been 61-61. Another election was one possibility.

The final figures for Moreton were known round Parliament House in a few seconds. Menzies had been quietly talking with two or three Party people and digested the welcome intelligence without moving from his seat. From corners in which they had been hidden ministers emerged joyfully. One of them, the usually sombre McEwen, leaped into the ante-room like a retired ballet dancer and hugged them all—not Menzies, of course, who sat quietly.

For two years the Government survived precariously and unexpectedly. Five times the Opposition tried to defeat the Government in Parliament and failed narrowly each time. Menzies had told his party that they could live dangerously and survive if they made survival their only objective. Personal antagonisms were put away. The rebels were as single-minded as the most acquiescent of the party, and, to their astonishment, they endured to fight the 1963 election on their own terms. "Nobody knows quite as well as I do how incredibly difficult living on a knife-edge is," said Menzies.

High on the list of credits was, as has been noted, his timing, a sixth sense not given to all politicians. Although it strangely deserted him in 1961, it had guided him through many vicissitudes since 1949. Usually cautious and conservative, he knew when to attack both in debate and in forcing an election. The flair was a combination of intelligence and intuition. Presented with an awkward problem, he often appeared to retreat from it. In fact, he was looking at it from every side and measuring courses of action. Having completed his analysis, he very often allowed his political intuition to dictate the timing.

Any assessment of Menzies as a political leader seems to provoke argument. There are the flushed partisans who say that he would have been properly cast out but for the Labor

I

split and the D.L.P. There are those who say that his conservatism was bad for an Australia developing like mad. Others say that he looked too nostalgically to England and Europe and too little at Asia. In one department of policy, however, his talents were esteemed almost without reservation by friend and enemy. We move now to an expert area, a kind of workshop territory, to look at Menzies as a professional.

III

The Professional

PRIME MINISTER Menzies sat at his desk in his office in Parliament House glancing over a pamphlet presenting one of his speeches. The young man sitting on the other side of the desk had edited the pamphlet and thought Menzies might care to see it. Like other innocents, he believed Menzies when he lightly said that he had little time to read newspapers and other lesser printed material.

Menzies dropped the pamphlet and gazed broodingly at the young man.

"I observed an error," he said.

"What was that, sir?"

"I did not use the word 'climacteric'."

The young man was not wholly unprepared. "It was 'climacteric' in the text, sir."

"Well, the text was wrong, my boy. I said 'climactic', I was not talking about the menopause."

Menzies was so fastidious about words, his words, that he rarely permitted anyone to write a line for him. His professional opinion was that a politician should be competent to express himself in his own idiom. He knew that ghosted writings and speeches could not persuade like a man's own words. Drafts submitted to him would be shudderingly put aside.

He deliberately mastered the art of speech, understanding that it is the politician's most potent instrument. He knew that ideas do not sell themselves, and have to be conveyed to others lucidly and convincingly. He studied other people's methods while polishing his own. It is generally known that Winston Churchill wrote and read most of his own speeches. Menzies once saw him at work. The technique was unusual. Churchill dictated in a manner peculiarly his own. A stenographer, familiar with his method, sat in a corner at a silent typewriter. The great man strode up and down sampling and savouring words and phrases. He looked at them for meaning and listened to them for sound. Until he hit upon the right word or the right phrase he talked half to himself. Fastening upon the words he wanted, he spoke them loudly, and down they went on the silent typewriter.

To say that Churchill read his speeches must not be taken literally. He delivered what he had composed with such artistry and timing that he seemed to be speaking without even a note.

Although Menzies did not hear Lloyd George, a brilliant and magnetic speaker, he discovered that the Welsh orator's method was to write his speeches and memorize them, a rare talent.

Menzies himself wrote important formal statements for Parliament with a lead pencil in long-hand. He did not write debating speeches or public political speeches (except a policy speech) or after-dinner speeches. He assembled facts and ideas and made summarized notes and headings, but he did not prepare the actual words. Where precision was essential, he might write out a speech on international or economic affairs. This was against the grain and he did it as rarely as possible. He believed that the language of a speech was best dictated by the mood of the audience. Those close to him gave him plenty of elbow-room when he was preparing his mind for an important speech. For a few hours before speaking he was unapproachable; the speech was taking shape inside his head.

His careful preparation was matched by virtuosity in delivery. The clue to his style was timing, a technique of the theatre acquired by Menzies so authoritatively that a great actress once heard and saluted him. "What superb timing!" she said. "I had heard about your Prime Minister's quality as a speaker. It can be defined in one word—timing." In short, he used the pause in speaking like a man who had spent his life in the theatre.

He could dominate the House when the content of a speech matched the artistry of its delivery. If, as happened, the content was thinner than usual, his speaking technique could give colour and apparent significance to indifferent lines.

His preparation of a policy speech was a study in professionalism. Traditionally in Australia an election campaign is opened with policy speeches from the party leaders. Usually, these policy speeches outline a three-year programme, nominate the campaign issues, and set out broad reasons why a government or an Opposition should be returned. Mostly, they are dull documents. They are dull not only because of the material in them, but because they are very often the work of many hands.

Few party leaders write the whole of their policy speeches. Menzies was exceptional in writing every word.

First, he would ask for supporting material from ministers and departments. With this mass of indigestible prose he would retire to the Lodge for a long weekend. And he usually emerged with about 15,000 words. This was far too long for an hour's policy speech. Operation No. 2 was to cut the first draft to size and then to polish it.

In the days before broadcasting a policy speech could go on apparently for ever. Radio programmes dictated a time limit of one hour for most of Menzies' policy speeches. Not satisfied with reducing his speech to the sixty-minute time limit, based on something near ninety-five words a minute, he had every page of his reading script marked for time. Thus, at any point of his delivery he knew whether he was going too fast or too slow. He knew whether to sub-edit as he went along. Without exceptional technical skill, he could not have watched himself as he talked, and that's what it all meant.

No Australian party leader in modern times could prepare and deliver a policy speech with anything approaching Menzies' professional skill. Indeed, the average politician who has reached the giddy heights of leadership and is confronted, for the first time, with writing a policy speech, cries for help. A good policy speech, whether or not it wins an election, asks for close preparation, concentrated thought, direct and persuasive language. Menzies possessed many natural gifts for such an operation, but he also directed to the job all his ability as a professional.

He was caught in the spell of words. Their weight, meaning, and sound endlessly fascinated him. That's why he liked reading poetry. It was no affectation. On the contrary, he would sometimes take up a book of verse and read for a while, when he was about to prepare an important speech. He turned to poetry to sharpen his taste for words.

His mind was uncluttered; it worked like a beautiful machine. He could eliminate from it everything irrelevant when he came to study a problem. No matter how complex the matter, he could extract the essentials and present his findings with great lucidity and simplicity. When he bent his mind to a task he could assimilate what was important out of a vast amount of material. When he was in the mood for intense work he could devour monumental reports and completely master them. His prodigious memory made this kind of operation easier for him. He could summarize and sum up. This not only enabled him to speak to the point; it was invaluable in Cabinet discussions.

No doubt these talents, with which he was most liberally endowed, tended to make him impatient with minds that could not work as clearly and crisply as his. He was the more formidable because he had at his command the precise words for what had to be said.

It was always fascinating to watch him record a TV speech. He spoke from a few headline notes, having carefully rehearsed in his mind what he would say and how he would say it. If, for example, it was a fifteen-minute talk, he asked the floor manager only to give him a signal when he had about two minutes left. He never bothered about a full run-through of the talk. Once the cameras and the lighting were right and he was given the signal to start, Menzies began talking. He seemed to have an in-built clock. Smoothly and without any apparent anxieties about time, he talked. Invariably the closing section of the talk was unhurried and, when it was all over, everything that had to be said was said. The time-keeper would say, "That's fourteen minutes thirty-five seconds. Perfect." Menzies would rise slowly, pick up his single sheet of notes, gravely thank the floor staff, and depart. The performance never failed to astonish the TV professionals. In their experience, he was unique. The timing was always perfect, the talk never had to be repeated because of some lapse on Menzies' part. The words always came out beautifully. It seemed so simple, but, in fact, it was a highly professional operation.

He had verbal mannerisms. "Immense" was a word that cropped up with monotonous regularity. He would refer time and again to a "powerful speech" that he had made—and this was always intended to be self-deprecatory and provoked the expected laugh. It was a trick of his to write himself down, but the audience was to take this as jocularity.

If a political campaign may be looked at, tactically, as a military operation directed by a leader who selects his battlefield and determines the outcome with foresight and single-mindedness, Menzies deserved a marshal's baton. Temperamental like others who enjoyed supreme command, impatient when minor campaign defects affected him personally, and touchy as a chutney colonel if a junior officer suggested a variation in riding instructions, he was—in spite of mortal frailties—an admirable C-in-C. For this reason: he surveyed the field before joining battle, made his plans (and they were always simple), and never departed from them.

It was always a pleasure to discuss with him the details of a Federal campaign. Sometimes the preliminary talks between the Prime Minister and his advisers occurred months before the official opening of a campaign. Professionals who had worked with him for years understood the exercise. They knew how he liked to approach the problem; they knew the policy background; they saw the emerging issues; they had assessed the political climate. And so, they said, this is how we see the campaign. What they saw they put down in half a dozen short paragraphs. They didn't write a long report or compose a lecture. It was the stark ABC of a campaign theme.

Menzies would read the short paper two or three times. He might gaze for a few moments into some remote area of wisdom cut off from mortal sight. He would then focus his gaze on the professionals.

"I agree," he would say, or perhaps, "I agree, but I think we can drop that second paragraph."

A little time might then be spent on programme detail and machinery; but the great decision had been taken in a few minutes—a few minutes preceded by months of calculation by Menzies and by his advisers.

However, when he said, "I agree", that was the campaign. From then until polling day—and it could be months away—the programme was clear. He moved from point X to polling day without deviating from the determined course. And he expected everybody to be as single-minded.

The policy speeches were, of necessity, crowded documents, but his campaign speeches stated the theme crisply. With minor variations to suit local audiences, he repeated the campaign theme at every meeting. The words would be different, but the theme was constant. It ran through his radio talks and his TV programmes. Party literature, often prepared long before the actual campaign, told the same story. All this was possible because Menzies worked to a clear and simple plan understood by both the parliamentary party and the organization.

During the actual campaign, however, he was not a cold, unemotional director, pressing buttons. Having scientifically planned the Operation, he invited Menzies the artist to do the platform selling. In his exuberant years, he thoroughly enjoyed an election campaign. The challenge of a meeting stimulated him. He preferred a boisterous meeting and audiences also preferred that kind of meeting; many of his listeners came along to be entertained, not instructed. In the mood, he could entertain splendidly. If the meeting was critical, he would approach it like a highly-strung batsman, the type who is on edge for the first few overs and then hits up a century. Menzies would open tentatively, feel for his audience, sense its mood—and then he was away, confident, fluent, challenging.

He waited avidly for interjectors. They were not all as helpful as the woman who walked down the aisle, waving an umbrella, and crying out: "I wouldn't vote for you if you were the Archangel Gabriel."

Menzies' retort has been quoted often: "If I were the Archangel Gabriel, madam, I'm afraid you would not be in my constituency."

128

Characteristic was his answer to a boisterous interjector at a noisy coalfields meeting. "Tell us all you know, Bob—it won't take long!" Menzies waited for the laugh to subside and said: "I'll tell you everything we both know—it won't take any longer."

On tour, an exhausting business, he expected his travel and hotel arrangements to be immaculate. Perfection, of course, could not always be achieved. There was an occasion when his programme provided for an awkward air connection in a very modest plane between somewhere in Victoria and Hobart. During the flight, which was bumpy, Menzies discovered that a more direct and comfortable flight could have been arranged.

At Hobart airport a reception committee awaited him. Its members were strung out along the tarmac, headed by the State president of the party; at the end of this staggered row modestly stood the gentleman who had made the travel arrangements. Stalking from the plane, Menzies walked past the president and all the others. He stopped in front of the gentleman at the end, glared, and said, "How are you, you monument of ineptitude?" He then sauntered back to the others, smiling, urbane, chatty.

He had an actor's hostility to scene-stealers. He was the star. The spotlight was on him. Bit-players should know their place. The wretched fellow whose job was to introduce the Prime Minister was always instructed to be brief—five minutes at the most. It happened occasionally that the poor man would be carried up on a flight of words. Every second that exceeded the allotted span darkened the frown on the Prime Minister's brow. At the meeting's end any up-and-coming youngster who tried to turn a vote of thanks into a speech was for ever damned.

In his relations with newspapermen Menzies was neither easy nor professional. He could be charming and amiable with individual journalists, but he was not at ease with the Press as an institution or with journalists as a tribe. It is traditional, at the end of a Parliament, for the leaders to say nice things about one another, as, for example: "I am sure that everybody would want me to say that you cannot live, work, and have your being in the House without developing a certain strange affection even for the men who do their best to defeat you." That was Menzies, who was less charitable to the journalists. "I should like to say 'thank you' to our hereditary enemy in the Press gallery who sometimes think little of us and who sometimes have that sentiment warmly reciprocated."

He could be at his most sarcastic when talking in the House about newspapers. Commenting on a leading article, a critical article, he threw it away with these words: "One must not unduly attribute sense to some of these blurbs." And there was the time he mentioned a newspaper's "dyslogistic reference to myself—I warrant they misspell that word!"

Perhaps his attitude was shaped in those harsh days of his first prime ministership, a time when he could not open his newspapers without encountering a taunt or a criticism. Or perhaps his resentment of criticism soured his relations with newspapermen. It was certainly an unusual relationship. Most of his predecessors managed to preserve a harmonious association with journalists working in Canberra. Lyons got along excellently with them. Chifley was always bland and friendly. Curtin used his press conference with fine skill, developing the background and off-the-record techniques. Often he deliberately tried out a policy line at an off-the-record press conference. For him, it was a miniature straw poll. Menzies' successor, Harold Holt, enjoyed the most cordial and friendly relations with the Press Gallery. But with Menzies it was always a kind of armed neutrality.

A final, mellow word about his desire for perfection in the spoken word. There was a gay night in the 'fifties, a dinner of the Melbourne Scots, at which he was chairman. No speech-making preparations were required, for the toast of Scotland was to be given by the Governor-General, Lord Slim. Menzies had only to preside—and to propose the toast to the Haggis, a traditional and solemn performance. Long before the dinner one would have imagined that he was preparing for a first night with a star's script to master. "How was that?" or, "Is that right?" In the end he was apparently satisfied. When the time came and the Melbourne Scots were amiably discussing their Scotch, he stood up and did it perfectly and with, apparently, effortless ease:

> Fair fa' your honest, sonsie face,
> Great chieftain o' the pudding-race!
> Aboon them a' ye take your place,
>   Painch, tripe, or thairm:
> Weel are ye wordy o' a grace
>   As lang's my arm.*

---

* Sonsie, *jolly*. Painch, *paunch*. Thairm, *gut*.

Epilogue

EMPTY and ghostly out of session, Parliament House in session is as queer a place as you would find anywhere. Like a theatre, it offers its patrons two stages, the House and the Senate. Off-stage, as in legitimate theatrical establishments, one hears the gossip, the chatter about the stars and the bit-players. Under the one roof the ministers and back-benchers have their offices and their party rooms, and under the same roof the newsmen and the commentators and the political letter-writers are also housed. Talk, a trickle early in the morning, becomes a river in flood by mid-afternoon, and roars on into the night, carrying with it fact and fiction, debris and rubbish, rumour and speculation.

Greetings incline to be more searching than the "howdy" of the street or bar. "How are we going?", or "What's doing?" dispense with the familiar courtesies about the weather and other time-wasting conversational gambits. When the political sky is dark over one particular party an articulate senator might greet one of his colleagues thus: "I smell death and decay." A young member is being instructed in the facts of life by a cynical old-timer: "Don't bare your breast up here; somebody might poke a knife into it."

Alarms are sounded almost as frequently as division bells. The morning's panic has been succeeded by another in the afternoon. Crises are normal. Blood pressures rise and fall. Tablets for nervous dyspepsia are rapidly swallowed. Gentlemen with flushed faces pass gentlemen with pale faces.

A veteran of the Press Gallery observes the comings and goings in King's Hall. "Look at them," he says, "always in a fidget. What they must have, above everything else, is strong leadership. They may buck, but they must have it. Without strong leadership, they run around like headless chooks."

No mood, no situation is sustained for long. A crisis in the

House does not remain at a critical point for long. Although the manner in which business is ordered contributes to this, the ingrained habits of parliamentarians deflate passions if they are kept high for too long.

Climax is sometimes followed by grotesque anti-climax. For a classic example of this one goes back to the perilous month of May in 1942. Australia was still menaced by invasion. Control of the South-west Pacific area was in dispute. For some days early in May wartime Canberra was full of rumours about a fateful meeting between American and Japanese forces. Everybody felt that an encounter of tremendous importance was imminent. Questions were asked in the House.

On the afternoon of 8th May Prime Minister Curtin walked quietly into the House as the day's proceedings were about to end. He looked very tense. Before he stood up to speak the members sensed his mood. Always tightly controlled, he had the habit, when angry or under stress, to prelude a speech by throwing down a pencil on the pad in front of him. This was the only gesture he made as he rose to move "that the House do now adjourn."

His statement was short, but it was delivered with extra-ordinary effect. Every eye was on Curtin. There was not a sound in the House except his voice.

"I have received a communique from the Commander-in-Chief of the Allied Forces in the South-west Pacific area stating that a great naval battle is proceeding in the south-west Pacific zone," he said. "This battle arises from the operations which began on May 4 and to which I referred in the House this morning. The events that are taking place today are of crucial importance to the whole conduct of the war in this theatre. I have no information as to how the engagement is developing, but I should like the nation to be assured that there will be, on the part of our forces and of American forces, that devotion to duty which is characteristic of the naval and air forces of the United States of America, Great Britain and the Commonwealth.

"I should add that, at this moment, nobody can tell what the result of the engagement may be. If it should go advan-tageously, we shall have cause for great gratitude and our position will then be somewhat clearer. But if we should not have the advantages from this battle for which we hope, all that confronts us is a sterner ordeal and a greater and graver responsibility.

"This battle will not decide the war; it will determine the immediate tactics which will be pursued by the Allied forces and by the common enemy. I ask the people of Australia, having regard to the grave consequences implicit in this engagement, to make a sober and realistic estimate of their duty to the nation. As I speak, those who are participating in the engagement, are conforming to the sternest discipline and are subjecting themselves with all that they have—it may be for many of them the last full measure of their devotion— to accomplish the increased safety and security of this territory. In the face of such an example, I feel that it is not asking too much of every citizen who today is being defended by these gallant men in that engagement, to regard himself as engaged in the second line of service to Australia. The front line needs the maximum support of every man and woman in the Commonwealth. With all the responsibility which I feel, which the Government feels, and which, I am sure, the Parliament as a whole shares, I put it to any man whom my words may reach, however they may reach him, that he owes it to those men, and to the future of the country, not to be stinting in what he will do now for Australia. Men are fighting for Australia today; those who are not fighting have no excuse for not working."

The battle the Prime Minister announced was the historic and decisive Coral Sea Battle. The silence in which Curtin had been heard continued for a moment. Then, in that curiously charged atmosphere, another voice was heard. Its owner was the member for Robertson (N.S.W.). He uttered a few perfunctory words about the Prime Minister's announcement, which still seemed to hang sombrely over the House, and then delivered these deathless words: "I desire now to refer to a scheme that was recently instituted by the Government in relation to the purchase for export for the next twelve months, of certain quantities of beef, lamb, mutton and pig meat. . . ."

The House, like the olive, is an acquired taste. . . .

Thursday, 20th January 1966, was quite a day in Parliament House. To see one Prime Minister bow out and another Prime Minister bow in was a most unusual spectacle even for the parliamentary lobbies, which had seen or imagined every conceivable political situation.

Strangely, it was a relatively quiet day. All the gossip about Menzies, when and how he would retire and who would succeed him, had exhausted itself. So, in a sober, quiet, calm atmosphere Menzies went about the business of departure. At 11 a.m. he announced his resignation to a joint party meeting. Then he resigned the leadership of the Liberal Party at a meeting of the parliamentary Liberal Party and saw Harold Holt elected in his place. He called on the Governor-General telling him of the resignation and recommending that Harold Holt should be commissioned to form a Ministry. Finally, he conducted his press and TV conference and talked about it all to the people.

This would seem an appropriate time to pull down the curtain on this story. The newspapers were full of it all. Millions looking at TV saw the dignified hail and farewell. Menzies himself had no wish to linger on the stage. But history is not so uncomplicated that one can select a particular day and say, "At eleven o'clock on the morning of 20th January an era ended." Like the seasons, men's affairs encroach upon one another. When the sun goes down, it is not night. There's an afterglow. All of which provokes an opinion that what has been called the Menzies era did not vanish completely into history when Sir Robert quitted Canberra; it ended when Harold Holt's life ended off Cheviot Beach a few days before the Christmas of 1967.

Is this too fanciful an idea? Menzies and Holt were dissimilar in appearance, in temperament, in outlook. The methods of the one were not those of the other. From the day Holt took over the very atmosphere of Parliament House was different. Commentators wrote about the end of one era, the beginning of another.

Why, then, the conceit that the Menzies period, or the afterglow of the period, ended when night fell on that tragic December night in 1967?

First, the transition from the Menzies leadership to that of Harold Holt was achieved smoothly and painlessly. Indeed, Labor parliamentarians, who do things differently, rubbed their eyes. That a change in leadership could be managed in a few minutes and with no fuss smacked almost of sleight-of-hand to Labor men familiar with savage fights for party leadership. Harold's Holt's accession to the Liberal Party leadership was unchallenged. Earlier, there had been talk in the lobbies about "possibilities" for the leadership. This happened while Menzies' retirement was a matter for speculation. As the day of decision approached, however, there was no talk of any successor other than Harold Holt. It was also apparent that the purple had been draped around his shoulders by the leader.

Secondly, Holt's first Ministry was the old team. His advisers, in the main, were also men who had advised Menzies.

Thirdly, the men who had sought a place in the sun in the years of Menzies' supremacy remained in eclipse. A contested leadership might have given them an opportunity to organize and to lobby. In the event, however, the change-over had about it something of a dynastic succession.

Outwardly, and in areas of high policy, the change from Menzies to Holt was conspicuous. Yet many of the consequences of Menzies' departure that might have been anticipated in January 1966 did not occur until Harold Holt's death.

Let us now look more closely on the seventeenth Prime Minister of Australia, a man who, although he appeared to conform to the average more than most political leaders, was, in fact, an individualist with rare and unexpected qualities.

In the second year of Holt's prime ministership, one of those difficult periods that perplex and tantalize all governments, a Liberal back-bencher, who had been converted from scepticism to affection and respect, said in his own sardonic way, "He's too naïve. He thinks well of people. He doesn't seem to understand that he is living in a jungle."

The nature of politics brings out in its practitioners some of the less lovable of human qualities. It does not, for example, inspire excessive trust. It encourages its initiates to look over their shoulders. Fostering group loyalties, it makes the doubting Thomas more doubtful about the infinite goodness of men and women.

Thus, it is basic to an understanding of Harold Holt to know that, in fact, he did see all people through rose-tinted spectacles. He seemed quite incapable of saying an unkind word about anybody. In the whole of Canberra it would be difficult to discover a man who ever recalled hearing Holt say anything personally hurtful. This, in itself, made him unique.

"Harold can charm the birds from the trees," Menzies said. But Holt's charm was not used with deliberate intent. It was not a political weapon; it was as much a part of him as his kindliness. If one can say that men liked him and that women adored him, it is more significant to say that children would joyfully clamber on his knees.

His amiability helped to make him the friendly chairman of a ministerial team and an easy man in control of party meetings. These roles, of course, cannot be explained in such simple terms. He had firm ideas about leadership before he took command. "Leadership can take various forms," he told an interviewer a few days before he was commissioned. "There is the type of leadership which is so far out in front of the team that there is danger of lack of co-operation, lack of warmth and some loss of effectiveness. There is the leadership which can lead but, at the same time, be close enough to the team to be part of it and be on the basis of friendly co-operation. I will make that my technique of leadership."

The same interviewer asked Holt whether he regarded himself as a "quietist" or an "activist". "Oh," said the new leader, "I think I can claim to be an activist. If you've had any other impression it could be because for many years I was lieutenant to a very strong captain. . . ."

Those years of deliberate reticence deceived those who, recognizing the gentler side of his nature, did not realize that he was determined sometimes to the point of obstinacy, that he was physically and spiritually tough, and that, when he had fixed on a course, he was tenacious and persistent. The rounded character was seen only when the curious observer recognized under the smiling exterior the strength and tenacity of a professional politician whose convictions, although simple, were strongly held and whose integrity was never questioned.

There was some who said that Holt would not for a long time, if ever, emerge from the gigantic shadow cast by Menzies. These prophets must have been confounded within forty-eight hours. Holt, a public relations "natural", had done his preparatory work so well that Menzies had hardly time to disappear into the wings before the spotlight of discovery fell on the new leader. His story from cradle time was told in every newspaper and on every screen. Australia saw him at Portsea, in his office, in his underwater gear, in impeccable suit, and in slacks and shirt. They saw him surrounded by a laughing, gay Zara and an exotic, slim escort of daughters-in-law. It was all very new and very modern. The new man had not only arrived; he had arrived in vista vision and rainbow colours.

In a twinkling, so it seemed, the suburban Lodge at Canberra, comfortable and sedate, burst into colour. Wallpapers that would have delighted the Prince Regent at the Brighton Pavilion and bedrooms that looked like a piece of pink Paris startled and delighted visitors. Modern pictures looked down enigmatically from walls that had so recently supported gum-trees on canvas.

Prime Minister Holt was certainly an "activist". He didn't fly so high as the astronauts, but he appeared to move nearly as fast, from one Asian country to another, to the White House, and to London. If Harold Holt made a new discovery of Asia, the Asians discovered Harold Holt and those who met him liked him. They liked him because he was frankly on a voyage of discovery. Strange people and strange cultures excited him, for he was a man with a great zest for life and for people. In the United States, of course, a burdened President found in Harold Holt's single-mindedness and loyalty a champagne quality.

The most remarkable, single event of his short prime ministership was the Federal election of 1966. With his instinctive political sense to guide him, he put national service and Vietnam on the line. There we are and there we stand, he said; and I want your support. He was given a record majority.

Twelve months earlier the pessimists said the new man would be lucky if he could hang on to the Government's 1963 majority. The old wizard had gone. What could Harold be expected to do? Heads shook, tongues wagged. But the election of 26th November 1966 was a landslide.

There is a story—and it may only be a story—that he once said, "I'll never be sixty." He was fifty-nine when he died. Perhaps he did have a premonition, because nobody could have crowded more into one life. He regarded sleep as a waste of time. He worked hard and he played hard. It was typical that, after hearing a TV panel debate the question, "What is the greatest fear in life?" he said: "One of them got it right. He placed fear of failure as the greatest fear of all. Fear of failure, I completely agree."

The thought of old age and the infirmities of old age was repugnant; to be young in body and mind was a kind of Greek ideal in front of him. Between his bout working he worked hard keeping himself fit. Yet the discovery of the world under the sea came relatively late in his life, although its effect on him was remarkable. It was not only an escape from telephones and the demands of office. Nor was it wholly a means of restoring his energy for the daily grind. He enjoyed the sport of hunting gigantic crayfish and he relished them on the plate. But the discovery had its stranger side. The challenge of the sea caught him. More profoundly, however, he was lured by an exotic world with Keatsian overtones of magic casements and perilous seas.

So those close to him saw two personalities. In Canberra, homeward bound, he leaned as he carried that legendary brief-case, a gargantuan case like a mobile office. It was crammed with papers. Occasionally, a zealous secretary would lay hands on the brief-case, sorting out the papers and digging out of some remote recess a piece of dry cheese dropped into the case on a flight, or a couple of broken biscuits. At weekends, or on those occasional visits to the tropical seas, he was a shining black figure, goggle-eyed, as he vanished under the sea.

On the morning of Sunday, 17th December 1967, he vanished for ever. He disappeared in the turbulence of a king tide on the turn in that dangerous Cheviot Bay that he knew like the back of his hand. Seen swimming in one moment, he was plucked away in the next by who knows what violence of sea or reef. It was swift, final, and, in an odd way, eerie.

Looking back, one finds it difficult to resist the feeling that there was something curiously inevitable about it all. Harold Holt, infatuated by the sea, was not a powerful swimmer. He knew that his mistress was capricious, cruel, and devouring. And it ended that way.

Five days later a Memorial Service was held in St Paul's Cathedral, Melbourne. Prince Charles was there, President Johnson, many distinguished Asian leaders, and Australians from every part of the Commonwealth. Sir Robert Menzies was there too. When the service ended and the crowds went their ways, it is unlikely that Sir Robert, brooding over his lost friend and loyal companion, realized that now, and finally, a political chapter had closed and a period in our affairs ended.

Index